PERSPECTIVAS
Hispanic Ministry

PERSPECTIVAS
Hispanic Ministry

Allan Figueroa Deck

Yolanda Tarango

Timothy M. Matovina

Sheed & Ward
Kansas City

Sheed & Ward™ is a service of The National Catholic Reporter
Publishing Company.

————————————◆————————————
Library of Congress Cataloguing-in-Publication Data
Perspectivas : Hispanic ministry / [edited by] Allan Figueroa
Deck, Yolanda Tarango, Timothy M. Matovina.
    p.   cm.
   ISBN 1-55612-770-7 (pbk. : alk. paper)
   1. Church work with Hispanic Americans. 2. Hispanic
American Catholics—Religious life and customs. 3. Sociology,
Christian (Catholic) 4. Christianity and culture—United States.
I. Deck, Allan Figueroa, 1945-   . II. Tarango, Yolanda.
III. Matovina, Timothy M., 1955-   .
BV4468.2.H57M56 1995
282ʹ.73ʹ08968—dc20   95-8617
                                    CIP
————————————◆————————————

Published by: Sheed & Ward
               115 E. Armour Blvd.
               P.O. Box 419492
               Kansas City, MO 64141

To order, call: (800) 333-7373

Contents

In memory of
Joseph P. Fitzpatrick, S.J.
(1913-1995)

Preface

The genesis of this book is the deepening reflection on Hispanic ministry in the United States in the decade since the 1985 *Tercer Encuentro Nacional Hispano de Pastoral.* Building on earlier works which achieved recognition for ministry among Latinos, more recent analysis probes the tensions, issues, and options facing the church as Hispanic ministry continues to develop.

This volume provides some essays from the past 10 years which reflect the ongoing analysis and new challenges in Hispanic ministry. These previously published essays are presented here in a single volume as a resource for pastoral agents. Collectively they illustrate the diversity of issues and perspectives in Hispanic ministry, as well as the diversity among the Latino population in the United States.

Some essays presented here are excerpts of longer articles; citations for each of the original publications are given in the accompanying bibliography. With the exception of a few minor editorial changes, each of the selections appears in its original form, including each author's usage of terms such as Latino/a, Hispanic, or more specific designations like Puerto Rican, Cuban, or Mexican American. This diverse terminology reflects the ongoing formation of group identities within the U.S. context.

Our thanks to the authors who allowed their articles to form part of this collection: Carmen María Cervantes, Kenneth G. Davis, J. Juan Díaz Vilar, Virgilio Elizondo, Angela Erevia, Joseph P. Fitzpatrick, Alex García-Rivera, Ada María Isasi-Díaz, Alicia C. Marill, Dolorita Martínez, Verónica Méndez, Arturo Pérez Rodríguez, Ana María Pineda, and Dominga Zapata. These essays first appeared in the following publications: *America, Catholic World, Christianity and Crisis, Concilium, Construyendo Nuestra Esperanza* (Saint Mary's Press), *Homiletic, The Modern Catholic Encyclopedia* (Liturgical Press), *El Mo-*

mento Católico (Claretian Publications), *New Theology Review*, *Religion Teacher's Journal*, *U.S. Catholic*, and *Vocations and Prayer*. All articles are reprinted with permission. For a detailed list of references, see Appendix Three: Sources.

Allan Figueroa Deck
Yolanda Tarango
Timothy M. Matovina

ONE

Models

Allan Figueroa Deck

F EW NEED TO BE CONVINCED ANY MORE THAT HISPANIC MINISTRY IS a major part of the U.S. Catholic Church's agenda for these closing years of the 20th century and surely well into the 21st. The *Tercer Encuentro Nacional de Pastoral* (Third National Pastoral Encounter) held in Washington, D.C., in 1985 was a palpable demonstration of how Hispanic ministry is a vital part of church life in every section of the country, not just in the traditional Hispanic enclaves of Los Angeles, New York, Miami and San Antonio. More than 1,100 mainly lay representatives of the nation's approximately 20 million Hispanic Catholics shared their hopes and frustrations for this once-marginalized sector of the church. The process leading up to the Encuentro had taken more than two years and involved hundreds of thousands of clergy, religious and laity in parish, diocesan and regional activities.

Shortly before the *Tercer Encuentro,* another noteworthy event had taken place: the selection of Roger M. Mahony as fourth Archbishop of Los Angeles. Archbishop Mahony assumed leadership of the nation's most populous and most Hispanic diocese. His entire priestly life has been spent in distinguished service to Hispanics at times when it was not as acceptable as it is today and in ways that were occasionally controversial. Archbishop Mahony speaks fluent Spanish and identifies with Hispanic causes, especially the struggle of migrant workers and the undocumented. His preparation for his new assignment was gained in the small rural diocese of Stockton, California, in the San Joaquín Valley where the needs of agricultural workers and the poor in general were given the highest priority. The decision to name

Archbishop Mahony to the Archdiocese of Los Angeles reaffirms the beginning of a new era for the church in the United States. A strong commitment to the service of minorities and the poor, along with serious concern about the causes of sociopolitical and economic injustices, are the hallmarks of a new generation of American prelates.

Given the recognition of Hispanic ministry, then, and the good will on the part of hierarchy, clergy and growing numbers of the laity of whatever cultural background, what are the tensions, the issues and options facing this part of the church as it moves toward maturity? There comes a time when the euphoria of having achieved recognition must give way to deeper insights and new challenges. Where do we begin?

At the risk of oversimplifying a complex reality, it seems useful, at least for the purposes of discussion, to characterize the various approaches currently taken in Hispanic ministry in the United States. There seem to be three recognizable schools of thought among the range of persons and groups involved in Hispanic ministry today. The first school is traditionalist in the sense that it simply tries to provide pastoral services more or less as the people have known them in their Hispanic country of origin. The second school is reformist in character. It desires to reach out to the Hispanic with a new message inspired by the Second Vatican Council. The third school is transformative in that it not only desires to reform but to bring about a radical change in the people's understanding of their faith and in the social structures in which they find themselves.

The first school—the traditionalist—is still at this point the largest and in many ways the most important. It stands to reason that the first step in any kind of ministry must be accepting the people as they are. Hispanics, by and large, especially the first generation in the United States, are rather traditional. The experience of being in a foreign land reinforces their need for recognizable institutions and traditional ways. This kind of ministry involves the majority of parish priests, women religious and lay ministers who are presently in the field. This approach continues to attract large numbers of people. Frequently, the work of dispensing the sacraments and dealing with the catechesis of children takes up most of the time and energy of pastoral ministers in this kind of situation. Ministers on this traditionalist wavelength sometimes feel that they do not get a great deal of support or understanding at the diocesan level, where personnel are frequently more attracted to the second school of thought, the reformist.

The reformist school of thought is especially frustrated by approaches at the parish level that take the form of sacramental dispensaries. Following the lead of Vatican II, these people are committed to a vision of the church that emphasizes personal responsibility. They realize that the vast majority of Hispanic Catholics in the United States have heard the words "Second Vatican Council" but know little or nothing about it. These pastoral agents are not interested in just "holding the fort"; they want to see changes in the level of the Hispanic communities' awareness (conscientization) and commitment. The notion of cultural Catholicism bothers them, and they want more than that for the Hispanic Catholic. This group also finds itself caught between the traditionalists and the transformationists. At times they seem unable to relate to either.

The transformationist group, the third group, inspired by Latin American theology, is convinced that an integral approach to salvation requires that radical sociopolitical and economic changes occur. The Gospel cannot be preached with credibility, these people believe, unless its ministers and preachers make a commitment to the integral liberation of humanity. For pastoral agents in this school of thought, sociopolitical praxis, sometimes including the notion of class struggle as it is understood in the Marxian tradition, is an essential tool of any authentic pastoral approach. Unlike the second group, which wants to see changes brought about specifically in the church, this group wants to see changes in society: jobs, decent housing, medical care, an end to discrimination and a radical change in the United States' role of promoting worldwide capitalism and the abuses that go with it, especially in the third world.

Underlying this third school of thought is the notion that the Kingdom of God begins here and now. Members of this group desire to do something practical to hasten its coming. They view the church as an instrument in that process, not as an end in itself.

There are negative and positive qualities in each school. The first school does succeed in creating a welcoming, familiar environment for the immigrants. It does, however, have difficulty with the sons and daughters of immigrants who know little about how things were done back home in Mexico, Cuba or Puerto Rico. Nor is this "business-as-usual" school very creative. Perhaps its greatest defect, however, is its frequent paternalism: The *padrecito* is supposed to know everything and do everything. This leads to a nonparticipative and passive kind of Catholicism. Along with this paternalism, there continues to be a lack of interest in service of others outside the limited fold of the parish, excessive sacramentalism and a corresponding disinterest in biblical orientations to prayer, worship and spirituality. The people themselves sometimes seem frustrated by this and continue to ask for more instruction in the Bible.

The reformist school represents some of the best currents in post-Vatican II Catholicism. It is reaching out to the Hispanic community with what it believes to be a balanced, modern approach. Its horizon continues to be the church itself, especially the parishes and some small Christian communities that it is striving to initiate. This group desires to form committed lay Catholics who are proud of their Hispanic heritage but are also critical of its unevangelized aspects; for example, sacraments without adequate preparation, paternalism, some discrimination against women and a dichotomous view of spiritual and temporal well-being. Members of this school want to be open to basic features of Hispanic Catholicism, such as popular religious expressions, but they continue to see superstition in many of these practices. This group is sometimes unaware of the excessively rationalistic bias of European and North American culture and its difficulty in dealing with ritual in almost any form.

The transformationists see the church as following the people in their historic struggle for social justice—something that has eluded so many Hispanic peoples up to now. Undoubtedly transformationists take the church's social teachings very seriously and are frustrated by the ignorance of so many in the church regarding this extensive and often radical body of official Catholic thought. Nevertheless, they lose interest at times in working within church structures. They see them as holding back and watering down the changes that necessarily must come about if the Kingdom of God is to become a reality. There can also arise a new "creeping clericalism" born of the zeal of priests or religious to strike a blow against injustice: they end up being the leaders instead of letting the laity lead.

Strangely enough, the transformationists can also resemble the members of fundamentalist sects. They doggedly insist on limited, sometimes quite literal, interpretations of Scripture. They are selective in their preference for the prophetic and a certain idea of the prophetic over the priestly and the kingly elements of Scripture. These transformationists have strict standards for acceptance. If one is committed to the struggle and of one mind with those who are "conscientized" and "committed," then one belongs; otherwise one is suspect. This is analogous to "being born again." Underlying some of the analyses made by this school is a kind of unanalyzed populism and a black-and-white, good-guys/bad-guys vision of the world.

It would be unfair, however, to fail to acknowledge the essential contribution made by pastoral agents imbued with the militant spirit of contemporary Latin American Catholicism. Their commitment to service of others, especially the poor and marginalized, counterbalances a kind of continuing ecclesial narcissism. Their effort to provide a comprehensive frame of reference for grasping the causes of so much misery in the world is absolutely necessary. If all so-called liberation theologians and their writings were to disappear tomorrow, these committed ministers would find plenty of fuel for their militancy in the words of Pope John Paul II himself. Perhaps their greatest defect, nevertheless, is found in the blurring of faith and ideology. Ideology of either the right or the left can keep people locked up in static, dull, interpretive frameworks. Faith, on the other hand, moves people toward self-transcendence and even new visions of where God is leading.

Ideology is also a problem for the reformist school. This is the ideology of the liberal middle class with its naive belief in the existing system's ability to meet the real needs of people with just a little tampering. The reformists' answer to social issues is found in the promotion of social welfare and not in any more radical change. In the context of diocese and parish, this group can be a powerful force promoting new programs and techniques. These programs and techniques, however, tend to be discreet activities unrelated to any comprehensive pastoral plan. In contrast, the transformationists are constantly calling for serious pastoral planning (*pastoral de conjunto*), by which they mean not just programs and techniques, but a comprehensive plan that combines goals and objectives and practical experience with a powerful vision of the future (a utopia) grounded on social analysis and theology. For them, new techniques without a theological vision are mere activism.

Many other points could be made and nuances given with regard to the complex issues discussed here. I hope that Hispanic ministry leaders will find some of these issues useful for further dialogue. It certainly is not my intention to denigrate the activities of any group in particular. Rather, by speaking with candor, it is my hope that better ways will be found, within the range of necessarily pluralistic options, to serve the Hispanic communities. One thing, nevertheless, is certain: Hispanic ministry is coming of age. As the debate goes on, the basic profile of the U. S. Catholic Church of the 21st century emerges. For what the Irish have been to the church in this century, the Hispanics will be in the next.

TWO

The Poor in a Middle-Class Church

Joseph P. Fitzpatrick

IT IS MY CONVICTION, AND THAT OF MANY OTHERS, THAT THE Catholic Church, now a middle-class institution, has not yet discovered an effective method of ministering to the poor. Difference of social class, much more than difference of culture, is the fundamental problem. But along with examining this problem, I would also like to mention briefly some hopeful signs of response by the church.

The Church of the Immigrants

Historians generally refer to the Catholic Church in the United States as the "church of the immigrants." Indeed it was. Between 1820 and 1920, more than 40 million immigrants, most of them Catholics, arrived. Thousands of priests, sisters and brothers came with them. Together with a dedicated laity, they founded parishes, organized dioceses and built and staffed thousands of Catholic schools, hospitals and charitable institutions. It was an extraordinary achievement.

Because of the church, the leadership of the clergy, the influence of the parish and the identification of the church with the poor as their advocate and defender, the poor moved into the mainstream of American middle-class life, and they brought the church with them. Its organizational characteristics, its activities, its style of life are typically American. The church came, poverty-stricken and persecuted, and, as we say of the immi-grants, we also say that the church "made it."

However, at the moment when the church might like to relax in comfortable middle-class status, millions of new arrivals are flocking into the parishes abandoned by the children and grandchildren of European immigrants. They are a new popula-tion—most of them Catholic, most of them very poor, most of them Hispanic. Once again the church is being challenged to be the "immigrant church" for the newcomers, to do for the Hispan-ics what it did for the poor and persecuted immigrants of the last century. But the scene has shifted. Despite the generous efforts the church has made for immigrants, the undocumented and the refugees, the church is not yet immersed in the lives of the new-comers as it was with the European immigrants. This is not be-cause of a difference of culture; it is because of a difference of class.

In the last century, the clergy and religious came out of the desperately poor families to which they later returned to minister. They were Irish or German priests from the poor Irish and Ger-man communities; later they were from Italian, Polish, Lithuanian and other communities. They were identified with the people they served; the Irish priests and religious came over on the converted lumber and fishing boats with the immigrants; many died in passage or in the quarantines where their people were confined. They knew the way their people felt, the sufferings they endured, the values they cherished, the practices that meant loyalty or generosity or devotion to the faith. They had a keen sense of the interests and needs of their people, not only relig-ious and spiritual, but economic, social and political.

When I was a boy, many rectory kitchens served as political clubs. They vibrated with sensitivity to the joys and sorrows, the frustrations or satisfactions of their people; because the poor were *their* people, there was an identity between them that was deep and strong and spontaneous. Archbishop John Hughes of New York was an immigrant himself; he marshaled his people behind him in the middle of the last century and overturned the Protestant political establishment by sheer political power. This is not, however, the situation of the clergy with Hispanics in many cases today.

The Hispanic Presence

To a large extent, American bishops, priests, religious and lay people of a variety of European ancestries are trying to minister to millions of a different cultural background and, in most cases, of a different social class. Many of these persons have made remarkable efforts to prepare themselves for this ministry. I know many of them, and I honor them. They have faced the challenge of learning the language and the cultural features of the Hispanic newcomers. Culture has come to be more clearly understood, and many efforts have been made to prepare priests, religious and laity for it. The second aspect of the challenge—namely, the class difference between clergy and the Hispanic poor—is, however, much more subtle. Many of the clergy are neither aware of it nor prepared for it.

Differences in social class are much more difficult to recognize, and much more difficult for the middle class to respect. I am aware that every social class develops a way of life of its own that can be called a culture—patterns of behavior that are taken for granted, that provide a sense of identity, psychosocial satisfaction and a sense of solidarity of the poor among themselves. But class differences become more immediately involved with economic and political interests, with conflicts of interest that can become irritating. Class in the United States touches the issues of power, wealth and education. The United States, unlike Latin America, is predominantly middle-class, and the church is middle-class within it. At the same time, large pockets of desperate poverty exist that cut across racial and ethnic differences. Poor educational achievement, lack of skills, inability to compete economically or politically, unemployment and reliance on public welfare are some of the features of the poorer class.

The Hispanic Poor

Hispanics are among the poorest populations of the United States. The Puerto Ricans—note that these are American-born citizens—are poorer than the blacks. In 1985, 42% of all Puerto Rican families in the United States were living in poverty; it was 30% for blacks; 25% for all Hispanics; for white, non-Hispanics, it was 11%. The U.S. bishops' letter, *Economic Justice For All: Social Teaching and the U.S. Economy* (1985), speaks severely about this. The bishops are emphatic about the need to enable these marginalized people to become part of the mainstream of economic, social and political life in the United States. They point out the difficulty of doing this—namely, the vested interest and control of power in the hands of the more affluent members of our American society. A large percentage of the poor are Hispanic Catholics; a large percentage of the affluent are also Catholic. How must this affluent middle-class—including the clergy—minister to poor Hispanics?

The bishops in their letter on the economy present a number of recommendations, largely relating to institutional and structural changes in the economy, and these are most important. Surely if the poor have access to much higher incomes, they will no longer be the poor.

The Immigrant Community

One integrates from a position of strength, not from a position of weakness; and it was the immigrant community that gave the immigrants of the last century the strength and stability to move steadily into the mainstream. And the heart of the immigrant community was the parish, in most cases, the national parish. The parish was the one institution in which everything was the same as it was in the old country: religious services in their own language and style; the same feast days and celebrations; familiar customs and practices that lit up the meaning of birth, marriage, illness and death. The cycle of life proceeded during the year exactly as it did in the old country. In a strange world it was the basis of their identity, their social satisfaction, their security, their strength.

The "national" or "language" parishes were often criticized as being divisive, as perpetuating old-world cultures in a world where newcomers should be seeking to become American as soon as possible. Actually, far from hindering adjustment to American life, the immigrant community and the immigrant parish gave the immigrants the stability and strength that enabled them to move gradually and with confidence into the mainstream of American life.

Whether with the national parish or without it, it is essential to assist the Hispanics to create a community of which the church is an integral part, where it serves as the heart of the community as it did for the immigrants of the last century. Ministry in their own language, in their own style, by clergy familiar with their cultural background is what the church demands. And to a large extent, this is what parishes and dioceses seek to provide.

But something more is needed: a penetration of the life of poor Hispanics by the church so that the church has the consciousness that these are our people, and the poor have the consciousness that this is their church. If the church can help the Hispanics create that sense of community, a small oasis of the old cultural world in the midst of a strange land, a world in which they feel completely *en su casa*, there is a possibility that the church may begin to fulfill for the new immigrants the role that it played for the immigrants of the last century. When the church fails in this role, many immigrants are prompted to shift to the Pentecostal and store-front churches where everything makes sense to them in an environment in which they feel at home.

I do not want to exaggerate this. Many of the old territorial parishes have, over time, become completely Hispanic and operate very much like a national parish. Some of these parishes are remarkable models that could well be imitated. But in so many parishes, Hispanics, even with their sense of a folk identity as Catholics, do not feel that the church permeates their lives in the same way the immigrants of the last century felt it.

I am painfully aware of rushing through difficult and controversial issues. But if we can really constitute the immigrant community, this will be the "position of strength" from which Hispanic Catholics, old-timers or newly arrived, will move with confidence into their rightful place in American society.

Hispanic Achievements

This is the challenge. The response of the church has been enormous, and achievements have been impressive. In 1957, Cardinal Francis Spellman established the Institute of Intercultural

Communication in Ponce, Puerto Rico, where in 15 years, thousands of priests, religious and laity were prepared for ministry to Puerto Ricans on the mainland. The Mexican American Cultural Center in San Antonio, Tex., is another impressive example. There probably has never been a time in the church when host dioceses have gone to such great efforts to receive newcomers of different languages and cultural backgrounds.

The church has institutionalized this apostolate. The U.S. bishops have established the Secretariat for Hispanic Affairs in Washington; regional centers exist in various parts of the United States. Most dioceses in which large numbers of Hispanics reside have established offices for the Hispanic apostolate. The bishops issued their pastoral letter, *The Hispanic Presence: Challenge and Commitment* (1983), and more recently, the *National Pastoral Plan for Hispanic Ministry* (1987). It would seem that these efforts should have resulted in great gains, but the gains have been much less than one would expect. The problem is social class. Generous efforts have been handicapped by the difficulty that middle-class Catholics have in identifying with the poor.

THREE

Caribbean Contribution

Dominga Zapata

"Could anything good come out of Galilee?"
(John 1:46)

THE GALILEANS HAD A REPUTATION OF BEING INFERIOR AND WERE depicted as poor speakers (Virgilio Elizondo, *Galilean Journey: The Mexican-American Promise,* New York: Orbis, 1983). In choosing to be one of them, God's Son took on himself this burden. Throughout history this identification of God with the poor, rejected, marginalized and seemingly ignorant people has continued to be part of the struggle of those who claim to believe. We have created other images of God that are more comfortable to accept and which require no conversion on the part of believers from a dominant, controlling and powerful society.

The Galilean is present in our land today. It may be as difficult to recognize and accept him as it was for believers during the time of Jesus. What good can a believer from a non-white, non-English-speaking, non-middle class and non-educated background offer the dominant church? Jesus' rejection was not primarily from those who did not know about the promise of his coming, about the promises of Yahweh, about the certainty of God's presence among the widows, the orphans and the poor. The rejection came from those who proclaimed all these truths about Yahweh as part of their beliefs.

Minorities in the United States have been stereotyped and identified with negative (what they are not) contributions rather than with positive (what they are) contributions. The image of the poor is often that of dependency, total need, incapacity to give and inability to understand the interrelationship of what is happening in the world around them and their specific situation of poverty. In other words, the poor person, like the Galilean, has been denied his or her reality as a result of the stereotyping of those who claim to control their destiny. They are considered unable to give or to contribute; they are allowed only to receive.

Puerto Ricans are part of those minorities in the United States whose contributions have been overshadowed by negative stereotypes, such as that all Puerto Ricans always carry knives, live off welfare, are drug addicts, etc.

It is my hope that reflection on the Caribbean Hispanic contribution may help non-Hispanic readers to appreciate the positive cultural and religious contributions of the Puerto Ricans to the church and to this country. Frequently these are overshadowed by the negative images of Hispanics in general, and Puerto Ricans in particular, which are perpetuated in society and unquestioned, even by believers. Christians today are being challenged and renewed, and are learning healing ways of viewing others.

Historical and Cultural Identity

Puerto Ricans are the second largest Hispanic group in the United States, making up 14% of the Hispanic population. Even though the majority are in the northeast region of the country, they are found in each of the 50 states. Their identity is intimately related to their history. Puerto Rico was named Borinquén by the Taino Indians (thus the familiar name of Boricua for Puerto Ricans); the Spanish conquistadors called it San Juan Bautista at first, and later Puerto Rico; and the North Americans called the island Porto Rico. Puerto Rico was eventually reclaimed as its official name, but Borinquén (the land of the valiant lord) remains the root identity of Puerto Ricans.

Pedro Mejias, a mulatto from Spanish and African parents, and Luisa, a Taina Indian, parented this new people rooted in the Taino, African and Spanish cultures. The African influence is present in the language, crafts, music, religion, entertainment, cooking, use of herbs and healing practices in Puerto Rico.

Through the "danza" and the "plena," the African influence made the Spanish music typically Puerto Rican. Communal celebrations (Areytos) of the Tainos became a strong part of the way Puerto Ricans celebrate as a people, a community, a family.

Most of the names of the cities are Taino. Spanish language and culture dominated the newly developing people, despite the fact that they were never the majority in the Island. And a form of Christianity, though not perfect, influenced all aspects of the colonization.

Throughout history, the core identity of Puerto Ricans as mulatto racially and Hispanic culturally has been enriched by various ethnic groups coming into the Island: Spaniards, Latin Americans, French from Louisiana, Haitians, Chinese, Italians, Lebanese, Germans, Scots, Irish.

Puerto Ricans express their identity and pass on their traditions through music, dance and poetry. The extended families of the Island embody the deepest cultural values, such as personalism, relationships beyond social classes, responsibility, primacy of the spiritual, authority of the family over the individual as a socially defined person, hospitality and generosity. But the family also embodies seeds of cultural weakness, such as strong control over relationships (especially with regard to women), male domination over children and women, a masculinity primarily based on physical strength, male aggressiveness that includes freedom with and sexual control of women, and the inferiority of women.

The political and economic history of Puerto Rico is an important element in understanding the contribution of Puerto Ricans in the United States. In 1542 Borinquén was colonized by Spain, until 1898 when it became a U.S. colony. Forty-eight years passed before a native Boricua was appointed governor of the Island, and it was two more years before Borinquén would elect its own government. Not until 1952 did Puerto Rico have its own flag and national anthem. The political status of the Island as a Commonwealth has not been satisfactory to all its citizens; this remains central in the concerns of Puerto Rico today.

In a letter of January 1989, the Puerto Rican political parties said in one voice to President Bush, "The people of Puerto Rico have not been formally consulted by the United States of America as to their choice of their ultimate political status." In its

February 1990 Report, the 8th Day Center for Justice summarized the meaning of colonialism for Puerto Rico: 13% of the Island is controlled and used by the U.S. military (Puerto Rico has become the home of 13 U.S. military bases and two nuclear satellites); 90% of the industry is U.S.-owned and operated without the protection of U.S. environmental laws, and all profits are tax-free; any decision made by the Puerto Rican people is subject to veto by the U.S. Congress; though bound by U.S. laws, Puerto Ricans cannot vote in presidential elections.

The economy of the Island is directly interrelated to the political status of Puerto Rico. With the transfer of possession to the United States, Puerto Rico became economically dependent on its new colonizer. The means of economic production are not yet in the hands of Puerto Ricans. The pace of development has not been able to keep up with the population growth.

Despite all this, Puerto Ricans continue to refuse to become the "America of the Caribbean" and find their roots in the cultural identity of their history. Luis Muñoz Marin, the first elected Puerto Rican governor of the Island, echoed his father's admonition: "We are not North Americans, we are Puerto Ricans, because God so willed it and thus we also desire it." (Clara Rodríguez, *Puerto Ricans Born in the U.S.A.*, New York: Unwin-Hyman, 1989, 9).

Migration to the United States has been a direct result of the cultural, political and economic crisis of Puerto Ricans in their own land. The migration of the 80s is a result of the 40% unemployment rate of professionals on the Island.

Religious Identity

The religious identity of Puerto Ricans is deeply bound to their cultural identity. A brief reflection on their history will help in the understanding of the significant religious contributions of Puerto Ricans to the Catholic Church in the United States.

In spite of much syncretism, the religious practices of Puerto Ricans are mainly rooted in the Catholic faith of the Spanish missionaries. For Puerto Ricans, to be a Catholic is to belong to a Catholic *community*. It is a religion based on relationships. Relationships with the saints, with the Blessed Virgin Mary and with

Jesus are carried on in personal relationships with godparents, "compadres" and patron saints. It is a religion that develops around life rather than the temple or the official minister.

Traces of religious rites of the Tainos and the African slaves are mixed in with Catholic popular practices. This influence in Christian religiosity and Catholic worship is known as the native syncretism typical of the Caribbean.

The religious world of the Tainos was centered around the communal life of the tribe. Their practices were closer to those of the African slaves than to those of the Catholic practices of the colonizers. The slaves married the Indians and both married the Spanish. This racial and cultural heritage is also part of the religious world of Puerto Ricans.

Many elements of the religion of the slaves continue to be part of the cultural religion of Puerto Ricans. Some examples are: the direct relationship between the natural and the supernatural, the sacred and the secular (the Supreme Being is known by instinct); the importance of relationship with the supernatural world through the spirits; the meaning of music in evoking and inviting the supernatural; the bonds between the world of the living and that of the dead; and the importance of participation in communal celebrations. In celebrations all are participants; there are no observers.

The integration of the Taino, the African slave and the Spanish colonizer have become intimately part of the religious experience of Puerto Ricans. Culture and religion have become inseparable. There are some popular beliefs with African roots that have become intimately part of popular Catholicism for Puerto Ricans: bad luck—belief that one could do harm to another through the spiritist; the evil eye—belief that the exterior physical energy could influence a person, even enough to kill the person (and that the wearing of an "azavache" can protect against the evil eye); reincarnation—belief of having previously seen and been in another place through the power of the spirits.

José Morales-Dorta gives several reasons why he considers spiritism and Pentecostalism as mental-health alternatives for the Puerto Rican community: institutionalized religion is too distant, too rigid and dogmatic to gain the faith and trust of the poor who need to unburden, to be listened to and to receive compassion. The small group offers security and a sense of belonging.

The leader is from the community and at the same level of academic formation. The small group offers progress based on faith and hard work. It demands meetings, almost always three times a week, facilitating intimate relationships centered on the sacred. The process of healing has a strong group or community significance. Thus spiritism becomes a warm and understanding unifier of a companionable and family experience. (José Morales-Dorta, *Puerto Rican Espiritismo: Religion and Psychotherapy*, New York: Vantage, 1976, 7).

The Taino and African influences have enabled Christianity to acquire its own characteristics in the Island. Religion is part of daily life. It continues to develop in the home rather than in the temple. Expressions of greeting or farewell (*Vaya con Dios; Que Dios te bendiga; Si Dios lo quiere*) include the religious dimension, inseparable from the cultural.

The religious value of relationships is carried out in the choice of "compadres" who become part of the extended family, with all the expectations and responsibilities. The community dimension is also strengthened by the many devotions and celebrations carried out in community. Death and suffering are accompanied by prolonged religious practices that support the family during the grieving period. These home religious practices have not been replaced by the funeral or commemorative Masses in the temple. Sacramentals (holy pictures, medals, holy water, rosaries, ashes, palms, etc.) are an important part of the religious practices.

Great feasts are public celebrations over and beyond previous participation in the church. Christmas, Holy Week, and celebrations of the patron saints of each city are examples of this. These strengthen communal bonds and bring forth an identity—a strong sense of belonging and of family in a socio-religious atmosphere of a people.

Pastoral Conclusions

The Catholic Church continues to be the institution closest to a people whose identity is integral to their Catholic identity. For the majority of Puerto Ricans who came to the United States before Vatican Council II, to be Catholic was primarily to be baptized and to belong to a Catholic people, a cultural religion. The experience in the U.S. has given them a more direct relationship with the life of the church, more participation in and an active awareness of the Catholic faith. But this new experience has been shaped by the deep religious roots of a history which is their own.

It is precisely out of this context that the contribution of the Puerto Rican community to the U.S. Church is made. To be a Puerto Rican Catholic in the United States is both a personal and an ecclesial challenge. The Catholic Church as a divine and human institution has been shaped by the history of previous immigrants in the United States. But for many centuries it seems to have deviated from its essential mission, becoming too identified with the dominant culture. It does not seem to have had much influence in the values that have shaped economic, social and political principles in this country; it seems to have failed to educate millions of middle-class Americans to be the light and salt of this society; it seems to have become comfortable with having its institutions be for its own kind. Thus the church seems to have taken on the same shape, form, language and lifestyle of the majority of its members who, though previously poor, are now part of the dominant society of America.

Puerto Ricans and other Hispanics present a challenge, often taken as a threat, to the Catholic Church in the United States. Within the history of Puerto Ricans in the U.S., that of the Catholic Church and the present dominant society, what contributions do Puerto Ricans make? These contributions cannot be measured solely by those offered directly to the life of the church because the church exists in relationship to that world in which it finds itself.

Given the negative stereotypes in society and the socio-economic situation in which Puerto Ricans find themselves in the U.S., the positive values and the contributions of Puerto Ricans can easily be ignored or passed over unnoticed. Despite these handicaps, the Boricua has found a way to be and to contribute from the mainland. Notable among these are: Pedro Pietri, Puerto Rican poet who has been able to express the sentiments of his people; Rene Marques, who portrays the vivid reality through the pessimism of Puerto Rican literature; José García, honored for his film "Down These Mean Streets," which depicts the destiny of the young Puerto Rican obliged to walk the painful streets of oppression in New York City; Jesús María Sanroma, famous soloist with the Boston Symphony; and many others who through their artistic talents have contributed to this country's cultural development, and who have awakened the consciousness of a people seeking their identity from the reality of the mainland.

Then there are the contributions to the life of the church. In a church marked by a history of racism, Puerto Ricans help the church minister more effectively to this reality. They are white; they are black; they are neither of these. Their identity is not merely defined by race. As Boricuas, race is only one component in their identity. Puerto Ricans, as a people, bring to the church the universal presence of white, black, and mestizaje. Despite the fact that they are United States citizens, they suffer the same ethnic discrimination as do many non-Hispanics, the same racial discrimination as do blacks. They have been, with other citizens, at the front line of the defense of the country. If the church could receive the Puerto Rican contribution, it could offer it in turn to the larger society in need of healing the racist past.

The Puerto Rican brings into the life of the church a different way of communicating. Spanish, body language and symbols are the core of such difference. The Catholic Church in America is universal not only because of its theology but also because of its concrete existence. Perhaps in no other part of the world does the Catholic Church have such an opportunity to live to the full its universal claim. To a church that has assumed the expression of the dominant culture as its own, and at times as the only valid one, the Puerto Rican people contribute another part of its own identity—the holistic language of the African heritage. English alone cannot be supported by a church claiming to be universal. Language is to communicate, to break down isolation and barriers. This is needed also in the dominant culture. A liturgy dominated by words can be enriched by the spirit of Areytos, in which movements of the body, symbols, community, and sounds of African, Taino and Spanish instruments contribute to the lifting up of the spirit in prayer and worship. All of these contribute to the spontaneous and free-spirited response to the presence of the sacred.

In an aging church, the presence of young people is a contribution for the present and for the future. With a median age of 21 or less, Puerto Ricans are a ray of hope for the future of a church overly burdened with the present.

Other contributions are not so visible. "Personalismo," extended family, community and a strong sense of belonging mark the spirit of relationships of Puerto Ricans. *Donde come uno, comen dos* (where one eats, two can eat) expresses the hospitality which the Puerto Ricans bring to a society full of fears and mistrust in relationships. This is best lived in the efforts of small ecclesial communities that transform a parish from distant relationships to close and caring ones.

Even in today's hectic, consumerist society, Puerto Ricans have time for children and grandparents. And the Puerto Rican woman, out of her own suffering, stands strong in her attempt to keep the family somehow united, even when it has disintegrated. Sensitivity, care and sacrifice in caring for the young, the sick, and the old, rather than working for power and possessions, are her signs of hope for her people's future. She is the symbol of the way death is faced as an integral part of the human journey. The pain and separation are real but are felt, mourned and then let go. But the letting go is not a void. Relationships with the dead continue through a series of home rituals and remembrance.

The power over death of the Taino and the African slave was strengthened by the Christian belief in the resurrection. The spirit and "mistica" of the Areytos and the power of the African drums have made it possible for the Puerto Rican to not only surpass the pain of death but above all the pain of life. The hope of the suffering poor is the greatest contribution the church could receive today and in turn offer the suffering world.

The deepest contribution of the Puerto Ricans comes from the wounded relationships within themselves at home, in the community, in the church and in a world in which many have declared God dead.

To the church, and through her to all of society, Puerto Ricans can say with Peter:

"Silver and gold I have not, but what I have I give to you." (Acts 3:6)

FOUR

Pluralism

Ada María Isasi-Díaz

THE TWENTY-FIRST CENTURY IS RAPIDLY APPROACHING AND WITH IT comes a definitive increase in the Hispanic population of the United States. We will soon be the most numerous ethnic "minority"—a minority that seems greatly problematic because a significant number of us, some of us would say the majority, behave differently from other immigrant groups in the United States.

Our unwillingness to jump into the melting pot; our insistence on maintaining our own language; our ongoing links with our countries of origin—due mostly to their geographic proximity and to the continuous flow of more Hispanics into the United States; and the fact that the largest groups of Hispanics, Mexican Americans and Puerto Ricans are geographically and politically an integral part of this country: these factors, among others, make us different. And the acceptance of that difference, which does not make us better or worse than other groups but simply different, has to be the starting point for understanding us. What follows is a kind of working paper, a guide toward reaching that starting point.

A preliminary note about terminology. What to call ourselves is an issue hotly debated in some segments of our communities. I use the term Hispanic because the majority of the communities I deal with include themselves in that term, though each and every one of us refers to ourselves according to our country of origin: Cubans, Puerto Ricans, Mexican Americans, etc. What I do wish to emphasize is that *"Latina/o"* does *not* have a more politicized or radical connotation than "Hispanic" among the majority of our communities. In my experience it is most often those outside our communities who insist on giving *Latina/o* such a connotation. The contrary, however, is true of the appellation, *"chicana/o,"* which does indicate a certain consciousness and political stance different from but not necessarily contrary to the one of those who call themselves Mexican Americans.

The way Hispanics participate in this society has to do not only with us, but also with U.S. history, economics, politics, and society. Indeed, that Hispanics are in this country at all is mostly due to U.S. policies and interests. Great numbers of Mexican Americans never moved to the United States. Instead, the border crossed *them* in 1848 when Mexico had to give up today's Southwest in the Treaty of Guadalupe-Hidalgo. The spoils of the Spanish American War at the end of the 19th century included Puerto Rico, where the United States had both military and economic interests. Without having any say, that nation was annexed by the United States.

Cuba suffered a somewhat similar fate. The United States sent troops to Cuba in the midst of its War of Independence against Spain. When Spain surrendered, the United States occupied Cuba as a military protectorate. And though Cuba became a free republic in 1902, the United States continued to maintain economic control and repeatedly intervened in Cuba's political affairs. It was, therefore, only reasonable that when Cubans had to leave their country, they felt they could and should find refuge here. The U.S. government accepted the Cuban refugees of the Castro regime, giving them economic aid and passing a special law making it easier for them to become residents and citizens.

As for more recent Hispanic immigrants, what can be said in a few lines about the constant manipulation by the United States of the economies and political processes of the different countries of Central America? The United States, therefore, has the moral responsibility to accept Salvadorans, Guatemalans, Hondurans, and other Central Americans who have to leave their countries because of political persecution or hunger. In short, the reasons Hispanics are in the United States are different from those of the earlier European immigrants, and the responsibility the United States has for our being here is vastly greater.

In spite of this difference, many people believe we Hispanics could have become as successful as the European immigrants. So why haven't we? For one thing, by the time Hispanics grew in numbers in the United States, the economy was no longer labor-intensive. Hispanics have lacked not "a strong back and a willingness to work," but the opportunity to capitalize on them. Then, unlike the European immigrants who went West and were able to buy land, Hispanics arrived here after homesteading had passed. But a more fundamental reason exists: racism. Hispanics are considered a nonwhite race, regardless of the fact that many of us are of the white race. Our ethnic difference has been officially construed as a racial difference: government, business, and school forms list "Hispanic" as one of the choices under the category *race*.

No possibility exists of understanding Hispanics and being in dialogue with us unless the short exposition just presented is studied and analyzed. The starting point for all dialogue is a profound respect for the other, and respect cannot flourish if the other is not known. A commitment to study the history of Hispanics in the United States—from the perspective of Hispanics and not only from the perspective presented in the standard textbooks of American history—must be the starting point in any attempt to understand Hispanics.

A second obstacle to dialogue is the prevalent insistence in this country that one American Way of Life exists, and it is the best way of life for everybody in the world. The melting pot concept has provided a framework in which assimilation is a must and plurality of cultures an impossibility. Hispanic culture is not seen as an enrichment but as a threat. Few understand that Hispanic culture provides for us, as other cultures do for other peoples, guidelines for conduct and relationships, a system of values, and institutions and power structures that allow us to function at our best. Our culture has been formed and will continue to be shaped by the historical happenings and the constant actions of our communities—communities in the United States that are influenced by what happens here as well as in our countries of origin.

It is only within our own culture that Hispanics can acquire a sense of belonging, of security, of dignity, and of participation. The ongoing attempts to minimize or to make our culture disappear will only create problems for the United States. They engender a low sense of identity that can lead us to nonhealthy extremes in our search for some self-esteem. For us, language is the main means of identification here in the United States. To speak Spanish, in public as well as in private, is a political act, a means of asserting who we are, an important way of struggling against assimilation. The different state laws that forbid speaking Spanish in official situations, or militate against bilingual education, function as an oppressive internal colonialism that ends up hurting U.S. society.

The majority of Hispanics are U.S. citizens who have lived here all of our lives. To engage with us, Americans belonging to the dominant group, as well as to different marginalized racial and ethnic groups, must be open to new possibilities, to new elements becoming part of the American Way. Above all, they must reach beyond the liberal insistence on individualism, now bordering on recalcitrant self-centeredness. This is all the more urgent given the importance of community and family in Hispanic culture. Community for us is so central that we understand personhood as necessarily including relationship with some form of community. Family has to do not only with those to whom we are immediately related or related only by blood; it is a multilayered structure constituted by all those who care, all those to whom we feel close, who share our interests, commitments, understandings, and to whom we will always remain faithful. This sense of family is closer to the model that is becoming prevalent in the United States instead of the now almost mythical nuclear family. Indeed, Hispanics have much to contribute to the changing concept of family in this society.

The importance of community also finds expression in the way we relate to others at our work places. Our business contacts and dealings have at their center personal relationships much more than institutionalized procedures and structures. It is often better to know someone, even someone who knows someone, than to present the best plan, have the highest bid, or be the first one there. And the very prosperous Hispanic businesses that do exist here, though limited in number when one considers that more than 22 million Hispanics live in this country, clearly show that the way we do business can also be successful.

Hispanics know that we wear our emotions pinned on our sleeves, that we express quite readily what we believe and feel. Not to feel deeply seems to us to diminish our sense of humanity. We do not find it valuable to hide our subjectivity behind a so-called objectivity and uniform ways of dealing with everyone. We proudly and quickly express our opinions. For us time is to be used to further and enjoy our sense of community. It is more important to wait for everyone to be present than to start a meeting exactly on time. It is more important to listen to everybody and to take time to dwell on the personal than to end a meeting on time.

And those who want to deal with Hispanics need to know that conscience plays a very prominent role in our lives because we live life intensely. We do not take anything lightly, whether it is play, work, love, or, unfortunately, hate. We often think in ethical terms even in inconsequential matters. This intensity and insistence on giving serious consideration to almost all aspects of life are a constitutive element of our high sense of honor, our way of talking about our standard of morality and personhood, which we are willing to defend no matter the cost.

Finally, those who wish to understand Hispanics need to know that our religious practices—what is often referred to as *religiosidad popular*—express our close relationship with the divine. A personal relationship with God and the living-out of that relationship in day-to-day life is much more important to us than establishing and maintaining relationships with church structures and going to church on Sundays. Christianity, and specifically Roman Catholicism, are an intrinsic part of Hispanic culture—something not always understood and taken into consideration in this secular culture. Many of the cultural traditions and customs still prevalent today in Hispanic communities are closely entwined with religious rituals. Processions, lighting candles, relating to the saints, arguing and bartering with God through *promesas*—all of these are not only a matter of religion but also a matter of culture.

The dominanat groups in U.S. society must acknowledge that Hispanics have much to contribute to the United States and that in order to do so we must be allowed to be who we are. Meanwhile, the dominant groups in society need to be open to cultural, religious, social, and even organizational pluralism. The nations that have failed and disappeared from the map of our world are not those that have been open to change but rather those that insist on rigidity, uniformity, and their own superiority. That is what should be adamantly opposed in the United States—not a multiplicity of languages, cultures, and customs.

FIVE

Multiculturalism as an Ideology

Allan Figueroa Deck

IN 1986 I PUBLISHED A PIECE IN *AMERICA* ENTITLED "HISPANIC Ministry Comes of Age" (5/17/86; see the first essay in this collection). In that article I pointed to a number of hopeful signs of development in the diverse areas of eccelesial, pastoral life called Hispanic ministry in the United States. The monumental pastoral planning process, the Third National Hispanic *Encuentro,* was on its way to completion and would shortly provide us with a *National Pastoral Plan for Hispanic Ministry* (1987). More Hispanic bishops had been named, and important non-Hispanic bishops, like Archbishop Roger M. Mahony in Los Angeles, were giving more priority to Hispanic ministry than ever before. Regional offices of Hispanic ministry were strategically deployed and diocesan Hispanic ministry offices were promoting all kinds of initiatives calculated to attract, serve and maintain ever-growing numbers of Hispanics in almost every part of the country.

Those of us who have followed the trajectory of this ministry over the past 15 to 20 years are now beginning to doubt that development or maturation is what is going on. We are beginning to think, rather, that things are unraveling. We are in a period of decline or, to use an overworked word, "crisis."

The complexity of the issues involved in this historic moment that I have characterized as the age of "the second wave," as my book on this subject is entitled, does not allow me to explain this crisis in any simple way. What I want to do here is state what some of us veterans of Hispanic ministry think the basic issues are. In doing so, nothing would please me more than to cause a storm of controversy. That would be a pleasant change from the silence, indifference, benign neglect or paternalistic "good will" that have too long characterized a great deal of the U.S. Catholic Church's response to this enormous challenge.

Why do I say there is a crisis? There are signs of it all around. Leaders in this ministry are getting older and they are frequently not being replaced. Services offered to the Hispanic communities at the basic level of parish are being maintained with difficulty or cut back. The same can be said for diocesan services. Regional offices of Hispanic ministry are being cut back or eliminated. Funds to implement the much-touted *National Pastoral Plan for Hispanic Ministry* were never allocated by the U.S. bishops. This is a factor in rendering the Third National *Encuentro* process a dead letter in many places throughout the U.S. church. Most Hispanics, and even most priests, still do not have the foggiest idea what it was all about. Over the years many promises have been made, faults acknowledged. But instead of following through and seriously evaluating what has been done, there is a tendency to introduce new titillations. Coherent, serious planning, execution of objectives and timely evaluation have not, unfortunately, characterized Hispanic ministry in most contexts. That is due, at least in part, to a failure to focus.

An instance of the malaise that grips Hispanic ministry at this juncture is the discussion about the appeal of evangelical sects. Recalling another article of mine, also in *America,* "Proselytism and Hispanic Catholics: How Long Can We Cry Wolf?" (12/10/88), I ask once more: How long can we cry wolf? A fascinating study authored by the University of San Francisco's Gerardo Marín and Raymond J. Gamba, *Expectations and Experiences of Hispanic Catholics and Converts to Protestantism,* recently confirmed what the Rev. Andrew M. Greeley and others have been saying: Almost 20% of Hispanics (in this case in San Francisco) have converted out of the Catholic Church since arriving in the United States. If, indeed, the major causes of this hemorrhaging of Hispanics to other religions are 1) the lack of ministers who speak the people's lingo and are imbued with real respect for their cultural ethos, 2) the lack of small, receptive, faith-sharing community contexts and 3) the lack of mission orientation in many Catholic parishes, then the task is clear: Target these deficiencies and take the means to deal with them. But for some reason we frequently do not target these needs nor take the real means to deal with them. Why?

We are told "there is no money." In pastoral affairs such an attitude has often struck me as bureaucratic, managerial and very suspicious. There is a catch-22 aspect to this, especially in the case of Hispanic ministry. Hispanics give generously to the church *when they know that the church is with them.* The key for the fundraiser is developing a healthy *personal* relationship with the people. Anyone familiar with funding and development in Hispanic countries knows that their standards are much different from ours in the United States. Works begin well *before* the money is in hand. They develop slowly. Some never are finished, but many do reach completion. *Seeing* the work actually moving forward is very important to Hispanics. Neat projections, drawings and plans leave them cold. They want to see the action. When they have their doubts, they withhold funding or drag their feet. A fundamental impasse occurs, then, when pastoral projects and decisions are predicated on "having the money." This is a cultural orientation, all very functional and rational. But Hispanics are different. One needs to "take a plunge" and commit oneself to them. Where managerial prudence dominates, the inherent risk factor in the church's divine mission can be suppressed. Hispanic ministry requires more than an ordinary ability to take risks. One must go in the people's door. The failure to grasp this means that pastoral planning gets hung up at basic levels over the issues of funding.

I have not the slightest doubt that working-class Hispanics could rebuild our decaying inner-city churches and schools, if they really thought that the churches and the schools were theirs. Not only that. They, like blue-collar workers of other times in U.S. church history, could build the church of the next century. It was the poor who built the church we presently have. It is the poor who will build the church of the years to come. Otherwise, it simply will not be built. It will only be maintained. There are signs that we are shifting into a singularly unimaginative maintenance mode. Our pusillanimous attitude toward the Hispanic challenge is at the heart of this syndrome.

Even more problematic is an attitude toward the exodus of Hispanics gaining currency in many quarters of the U.S. Catholic Church. I've even heard it from thoughtful theologians. It goes like this: "Hispanics are rather emotional and poor. The evangelicals like working with those kinds of people. This is an ecumenical period. Those evangelical sects are not so bad. So isn't it nice that the Hispanics are leaving the church? Surely they will be saved." The assumptions and implications of this line of reasoning are too vast to deal with here. My point is that we are being conditioned now to accept the massive departure of Hispanics from the church. Involved in this neat line of reasoning is, in my judgment, a terrible death wish. It is cause for alarm.

Another reason for the impasse in reaching out and effectively serving Hispanics goes much deeper than cultural differences on money matters, a lack of magnanimity or a morbid death wish. It has to do with the multicultural context that Hispanics and other third world peoples encounter in the United States and in the church. The church's leaders moved away from the national parish as an instrument of policy. It had been the fundamental and fabulously successful approach to the pastoral care of immigrants for more than 100 years. By 1945 the church experienced itself as mainstream. Bishops took advantage of the occasion to abandon a system that successfully delivered services to the teeming masses, but also caused all manner of conflict. National churches, identified with their people and presided over by committed pastors, were hard to control. They posed problems for bishops. Today we see the last vestiges of those old ethnic Catholic parishes in places like Detroit and Chicago. Hispanics and other recent immigrant groups have simply not been offered the national or personal parish option. That option, even though made easier now in the new Code of Canon Law, is not being taken. In its place we are promoting "multiculturalism."

While national parishes as developed in the last century are not, practically speaking, viable for a host of reasons, experiments with the concept of forming communities around ministers or leaders, whether priests or not, totally identified with a given language and cultural group, are possible. The circumstances call for experimentation with both the concept of parish, its structural arrangements and practical operations, as well as with the cultural focus of ministry. Some strategic planning going on in dioceses makes the large, efficient multicultural parish the paradigm of the future. This is a big mistake, for which archdioceses like Detroit and Chicago may eventually repent. It reduces options, deadens the imagination and forces the church into a mold that simply does not deal with differentiated, pastoral and cultural realities. These options are often diametrically opposed to what we thought we had learned about how not to proceed in Hispanic ministry.

The consequences of this historic move toward a multicultural approach have been devastating. What it means is that, in practice, the Hispanic communities do not find secure, inviting places of worship, nor ministers to go with them. In the name of the church's multicultural reality, a fundamental moment in outreach, one that takes time and tender, loving care, is short-circuited. People are sent to the large, multicultural parish that has two tracks or more and in some rare cases is "integrated." The sociological truth that people unite from a position of strength is in practice being negated by the multicultural ideology. The practical result of this is that only the most resourceful Hispanics are surviving in our parishes, while the ordinary people find little to nourish their faith, little that is recognizable in the well-intentioned but mistaken efforts to put multiculturalism above the particular cultures. This is a classic case of putting the cart before the horse.

An example that readily comes to mind is the bilingual or multilingual liturgy. Anyone who has worked on such affairs knows that it is not easy to execute such liturgies successfully. There seems to be a consensus that by no means should they become the norm, although an occasional one can be effective. Even more telling is the case of Holy Week. In the multicultural context the official liturgy, which is already quite complicated and difficult to celebrate, is burdened with patches from this and that culture. What results is sometimes unrecognizable. In the Hispanic context this is especially tragic since so much of the people's faith is concentrated in Holy Week as they traditionally have celebrated it. Even before the reform of the liturgy, Hispanics had developed their own popular way, and it co-exists with the official way. Among its more moving components are a dramatized Way of the Cross (*vía crucis*), an orgy of oratory called "The Seven Last Words" (*las siete palabras*) and "The Condolences (*pésame*) to the Virgin," as well as strategically placed processions. When energy is placed on the official liturgy and on its multicultural adaptation, there is little left for the people's liturgy. The result is a flat, unmoving and (for Hispanics) somewhat unrecognizable Holy Week.

The ideology of multiculturalism has even more devastating consequences. In an age of "strategic planning" it provides an excuse to close more churches. For the ideal is no longer struggling to relate to the particular, but going beyond it (miraculously) to some ideal state of unity expressed in the "multicultural context." Multiculturalism also allows some parishes, seminaries and houses of formation to ignore the particular cultures of their parishioners and students by substituting some vague, watered-down multicultural approach. Folkloric elements from a variety of cultures are juxtaposed. Exotic foods, music and dance are occasionally highlighted. The approach legitimates superficiality and even worse, it allows those who currently control parish, school, seminary or diocesan office to ignore the issue of culture in all its depth.

The ideology of multiculturalism also plays into certain dysfunctional tendencies found in religious institutions. One of them is the fear of conflict. The unspoken assumption is that conflict is always bad. Anyone familiar with cultural encounters knows that they are intense. Smoothing them over in the name of multiculturalism can be pathological. The result is that the stronger group, whose particular culture has historically had the upper hand, continues to have it. There is a fundamental inequality. Multiculturalism becomes a smokescreen.

That is precisely what we have seen time and time again within public education. Educators justify their failure to deal with the cultures of their students by providing a vague, multicultural curriculum. It frequently satisfies no one, but allows the deeper educational and linguistic issues to go ignored. Something similar, it seems to me, can happen in the church.

My remarks so far may be interpreted as showing little awareness of positive developments in Hispanic ministry occurring all over the country. I think I am aware of some of them. Certainly the program of home visitations and other forms of outreach being promoted in the Archdioceses of Newark and Los Angeles are new and exciting ventures long overdue. The Pastoral Plan to Combat Racism, implemented by Archbishop Rembert Weakland, O.S.B., of Milwaukee, is truly impressive for its sensitivity and perceptiveness. A lay ministry formation effort in the Diocese of El Paso, called the Tepeyac Institute, has provided hundreds of laity with an intense formation experience based on an innovative curriculum and pedagogy designed with Hispanics in view. In its own way, moreover, RENEW continues to have a powerful effect on Hispanics exposed to many of its dynamics. Here and there one hears of credible efforts to move ahead with the priorities of the *National Pastoral Plan for Hispanic Ministry,* especially its promotion of basic ecclesial communities. Some may point to the fact that there are more Hispanics than ever in seminaries, especially diocesan ones, and that this is a most hopeful sign. Vibrant charismatic groups, often marginal, misunderstood or even feared, continue to motivate thousands of Hispanics throughout the nation. *Cursillos* provide a similar service. Yes, there is some reason for hope. But these gains, such creativity and commitment can, and in too many instances are being emasculated by unanalyzed policies, opposition or inertia at the institutional level. The upshot of all this is that the church is diminished. It is not all that it could be.

An underlying cause for the current crisis in Hispanic ministry is the hegemony of a misguided understanding of multiculturalism, one that ultimately puts down and/or co-opts the Hispanic, black and other third world elements in the church. Understood correctly, multiculturalism is an exciting value. The presence of so many diverse cultures is a fantastic blessing for our nation and church. But authentic multiculturalism, like grace, does not come cheaply. The construction of an authentic multicultural society is a slow, delicate and often excruciating process, much like giving birth. There are signs, then, that the US. Catholic Church of the future, gestating now in the womb in the form of Hispanic new life, may be heading for a miscarriage.

No Melting Pot in Sight

Timothy M. Matovina

THE EXODUS FROM CATHOLIC "GHETTOS" IN THE YEARS FOLLOWING World War II is seen as a positive development by many Catholics in the United States. This perception often leads to the expectation that Hispanic Catholics will walk down the same path the others have trod before them, as is evidenced by statements like: "They'll integrate in another generation or so anyway. By offering services in Spanish, you're just holding them back. Other immigrant groups also felt 'put upon' when they first got here. This is just one more group going through the adjustment to American life. This too will pass."

Such statements are based on the mistaken contention that assimilation into the cultural milieu of the United States is inevitable for residents of this land, be they Hispanics or any other group. The continued insistence that Hispanics will soon pass through the assimilationist melting pot and "be American like us" is not only false, but also harmful for our Hispanic sisters and brothers, and thus for the church. There are at least seven differences between the situation of today's Hispanics and that of European Catholics who arrived during the great century of immigration (1820-1920).

Crossing el Rio, Crossing the Ocean

Perhaps the most important difference is the physical proximity of the countries from which Hispanics originate. Here it must be noted that many Hispanics are not recent immigrants, but have been here for generations. Others, such as Cubans and political refugees from Central America, are unable to return home at this time. Nonetheless, the fact remains that contact with the country of origin (and other countries where Spanish is spoken) is more frequent for today's Hispanic than for immigrants who crossed the ocean. Spanish television programs and improved transportation have added to the trend of greater contact with one's homeland and the larger Hispanic world. This contact reinforces language and culture and counteracts the effects of the melting pot.

Continuous Flow of Immigrants

One of the key factors in the cultural assimilation of German, Italian, Polish, Irish and other 19th-century Catholic immigrants was the legislation of 1924 that effectively curtailed further immigration. As the flow of first generation immigrants from each group waned, group acceptance of U.S. cultural values accelerated. Despite continuing efforts to restrict immigration, however, this pattern of declining immigration is not evident among Hispanics. A steady flow of new arrivals continuously reinforces language and culture and is a second important difference between today's Hispanics and yesterday's European Catholic immigrants.

Poverty

Another reason for the assimilation of European immigrant groups was the rise out of poverty to a better standard of living. This was particularly true in the years following World War II, when an unprecedented number of Catholics and others in the United States achieved middle-class status. For many, this financial success provided irrefutable evidence of the superiority of the American way. The move to the suburbs placed Catholics in ethnically and religiously mixed neighborhoods, further enhancing their identity as Americans and dissipating their ethnic consciousness.

Here again the situation of most Hispanics is decidedly different. When the provinces of northern Mexico were forcibly annexed through the wars with Texas (1835-36) and the United

States (1846-48), for example, the 80,000 Mexican citizens who remained in the conquered territory did not achieve greater financial prosperity. In fact, many were impoverished by the illegal confiscation of their lands. Today poverty continues to be the burden of many Hispanics and current economic trends suggest that the middle class will diminish rather than expand. Although there are exceptions, the rise to the middle class, which was so influential in the assimilation of other Catholics, is not occurring massively among Hispanics.

Racism

Even if material prosperity is realized, the issue of racism remains. It is with good reason that proponents of immigration reform have pointed to the symbolic irony that the Statue of Liberty faces Europe and has its back to Asia and Latin America. Hispanics are not alone in the experience of discrimination, of course. Almost every immigrant group had to endure some form of prejudice upon arriving in the United States. With Hispanics and other groups (most notably African Americans) from outside of Europe, there is frequently a critical difference, however: skin color. While white European immigrants could blend into mainstream American society once they knew the language and culture, the ethnic origin of most Hispanics remains readily apparent. Often subtle (and not so subtle) racist treatment is the result. Continuing racism leads Hispanics to band together for mutual support and to resist assimilation into a society perceived as unappreciative of the Hispanic presence.

Urbanization

Census figures of 1990 indicate that about 90% of Hispanics in the United States reside in urban areas. The pattern of living in urban enclaves is not without precedent among Catholic groups. Most of the Irish who came in the 19th and early 20th centuries lived in cities. Because of enduring racism and poverty, however, the tendency to live in urban clusters appears to be more persistent among Hispanics. Situated in what amounts to a transplanted San Salvador, Havana, San Juan, Mexico City, etc.,

Hispanic cultural patterns and the use of Spanish are reinforced and the effect of the melting pot is further neutralized.

Church Teaching on Cultural Adaptation in Ministry

Another difference between the situation of Hispanic Catholics today and that of 19th-century immigrant groups is the changing perspective on evangelization within the church. Pope Benedict XV's *Maximum Illud* (1919) was the first apostolic letter devoted exclusively to the church's missionary efforts in foreign lands. Subsequently, Pius XI, Pius XII and John XXIII promulgated encyclicals on the missions, and Vatican II issued the first conciliar document on this topic *(Ad Gentes)*. These magisterial statements evidence a growing awareness that Catholic evangelization has too often promoted Western culture as if it were intrinsic to the Gospel. Since the council the theme of adapting the proclamation of the Gospel to local cultures and customs has been further developed, *e.g.,* in Paul VI's apostolic exhortation *Evangelii Nuntiandi* (1975) and John Paul II's encyclicals *Slavorum Apostoli* (1985) and *Redemptoris Missio* (1990).

Hispanic theologians in the United States have pointed to the teaching on respect for culture in arguing that the image of the melting pot ought to be replaced by that of the stew pot. Just as in a stew pot each ingredient enriches and is enriched by the other ingredients, so too in our society the different cultures should be mutually enriching and should not overpower one another. Far from suggesting a mere superficial multiculturalism, the stew pot image ought to inspire the church in the United States to face the issue of culture in all its depth ("The Crisis of Hispanic Ministry: Multiculturalism as an Ideology" by Allan Figueroa Deck, *America*, 7/21/90; see the fifth essay in this collection). This vision of a pluralistic society has also been articulated by grass-roots Catholics through the three national Hispanic *Encuentros* (1972, 1977, 1985), as well as by the National Conference of Bishops in their pastoral letter *The Hispanic Presence: Challenge and Commitment* (1983) and the *National Pastoral Plan for Hispanic Ministry* (1987).

Seeing America as a stew pot rather than a melting pot has strengthened the efforts of many Hispanics consciously to resist assimilationist pressures. Unlike that of German Catholics and others of the last century who also attempted to resist assimilation, Hispanic resistance has been buttressed by the magisterial teaching and theological reflection that place such efforts within the Gospel imperative.

Persistence of Popular Religion

Hispanic American theologians have suggested that resistance to the melting pot is manifested in popular expressions of faith. The persistence of popular religion as a defense against the assault of assimilationist pressures is a further difference between the experience of today's Hispanics and that of European Catholics, whose cultural Catholicism faded with (or shortly after) assimilation. To the extent that popular expressions of faith continue to be practiced among Hispanics, group resistance to cultural assimilation will tend to be fortified.

This essay reflects the views expressed by Hispanic Catholic faithful, theologians and bishops over the past 20 years. Yet despite the numerous voices that have called for an end to an attachment to the melting pot, we as a church seem to be suffering from collective denial, from a refusal to hear anything except the naive claim that soon Hispanic Catholics will pass through the melting pot like others before them. This collective denial is the cause of much cultural insensitivity, poor pastoral planning and failure in Hispanic ministry. If acknowledgment of the truth about the melting pot became more common among us, our ministry with Hispanics would be greatly enhanced.

SEVEN

Women

Yolanda Tarango

As I REFLECT ON THE HISPANIC WOMAN AND HER ROLE IN THE church, a variety of images come to mind. I see the *viejitas,* those old women, whose wrinkled faces full of character speak volumes about faith and faithfulness. I think of the middle-aged grandmothers whose fundraising skills have built and sustained church institutions. I remember the pious women who have borne so much suffering but somehow find the strength to continue. I hear the concern of younger working mothers, worried about conveying a sense of Hispanic culture and religious traditions to their children. I also feel the pain of women who can no longer be at home in a church which they perceive as negating their full personhood and rejecting their contribution.

All of these images reflect the Hispanic woman, yet each embodies a different relationship to the church's life. My tendency, when addressing the topic of Hispanic women's role in the church, is to look to my mother and my grandmother and the heritage of "working in the church" that they left me. Their dedication to building the church has sustained me through many doubts and uncertainties. Yet, if this reflection is to be more than a nostalgic portrayal of Hispanic women, I must also take into consideration the experience of my peers. They are the Hispanic women who, with tremendous self-respect, are struggling not only for their own and their sisters' liberation but for a more inclusive church. It is important that we recognize the continuity between the work and dedication to the church of our foremothers and the struggles of Hispanic women who are questioning their role in the church today.

Our Foremothers/Nuestras Madres

Reflecting on the lives of women, symbolized by our mothers and grandmothers, can be empowering, not only as an inspiration but as a guide for grounding our faith and action. An examination of their lives would lead us to ask, what did church mean to them and how did they draw strength from it? Did they see themselves as having a specific role in the church or did that question even matter to them? As we delve into their story, seeking answers to these questions, perhaps we will begin to see some of the common threads of our experience.

For my grandmother and the Hispanic women of her age, church was perceived not so much as an institution but as a community. Church provided the legitimate social context in which Hispanics could gather as a group to express their faith. I feel I entered the church at my grandmother's side through the stories she would tell me of her childhood. These were usually narratives of family and communal events framed in liturgical celebrations, such as parish patronal feasts and holydays. When she described encounters with the official church, the men of my family were usually the principal actors. Many stories included accounts of my great-grandfather and uncles and their confrontations with the foreign priests in an effort to preserve cultural rituals. In these episodes women appear to have been merely passive observers. Yet, in her accounts of religious rituals and celebrations in the home, the women of the family always emerged as the central characters. My grandmother and the women of her generation exercised their religious leadership in the Hispanic community as healers, prayer leaders, and dispensers of blessings. They were also the main persons responsible for passing on the traditions. They did so in a uniquely female manner, teaching through stories, rituals, and example. These women perceived their religious role as fundamental. While the official church was understood, foremost, as possessing moral authority and having the power to convene the community, the women's role was securely established in popular religious practice, which has always been much more inclusive of female leadership.

Hispanic women of my mother's generation were more deeply impacted by the forces of assimilation as well as by the social and economic pressures of society. The rise in Hispanic "nuclear families" during this period was indicative of this phenomenon. Moving from the traditional, extended-family model was usually related to economic factors; families moving to the city, or to another city, in order to find a job left behind their support systems, which resulted in considerable pressure for women. They experienced greater isolation as well as increased responsibility for the emotional support of the family. Participation in the official church provided a harbor as well as an opportunity to remain close to a culturally familiar tradition, but it also encouraged the erosion of traditional religious customs. Going to church began to take precedence over being church in the home. This resulted in the loss of many religious traditions and practices. Yet, for many Hispanic women the church was survival. It offered the only space where they could dare to have hope in the midst of a harsh reality. It provided a sense of connectedness where a vacuum had been created by the loss of the extended family.

Another aspect of participating in the church for this generation was volunteer work. The voluntary services of women, especially in fundraising activities, were welcomed by the official church. Thus, Hispanic women functioned in the church even though they had no official status. The positive side of voluntary service in the church was that it provided an opportunity for women to work in an area outside of the home at a time when patriarchal structures did not allow other spaces for women to develop. For Hispanic women, this was the only arena in which they could legitimately, if indirectly, engage in developing themselves. Consequently, they became more dependent on the official church for their religious activity and more alienated from their former role in popular religion. Women of this generation perceived the church as the primary means to keep the family united and cultural values alive. Their work in the church was chiefly oriented towards building the community.

Hispanic Women Today/La Mujer Hispana Hoy

The women of my generation, with increased possibilities for education and self-development, saw our mothers' role in the church and expected to expand on it. Instead, we discovered that the church valued women's gifts only to the degree that they were placed at the service of specific and limited functions, usually on a volunteer basis. With the expansion of women's role in society, we no longer had the same need for legitimate activity outside of the home, nor the time to give to volunteering that our mothers had been able to give. The result has been that many of the tasks that women had traditionally performed as volunteers have become professionalized. Women's traditional mode of participating in the church, for the most part, no longer exists.

Hispanic women, who have always been identified with religious leadership in the community, have experienced a tremendous sense of loss with regard to our role in the church. Our grandmothers found their role in popular religion, our mothers in voluntary service to the parish, but neither of these roles are particularly relevant for Hispanic women today. A feeling of distance from the church has led many Hispanic women to question the church's ability to respond to their religious needs and expectations. Hispanic women are not abandoning the church, though they feel that the church has abandoned them. They are changing their expectations of what this institution can offer them. They are also seeking other ways to meet their religious needs. As one Hispanic woman recently told me, "At some point church ceased to be the place that nurtured us. . . . We are not satisfied with what the institutional church offers us. We have found God and support in people and in other women. We have re-discovered the community."

The rediscovery of community is the point of continuity. It is the return to our grandmother's experience of, and our mother's efforts for, church as community. Though women's work in the church has traditionally been of a community-building nature, this has often been frustrating because the structure of the official church is not a positive environment for community. Hierarchy and dualism choke the life out of it. Therefore, the strategy has been turned inside out. Instead of working to create community within the boundaries of the official church, women today are discovering and creating church in the larger community. This is what the "rediscovery" of community means.

The implications of Hispanic women rediscovering community outside of the church are broader than they may seem. The boundaries of the church are being stretched and its meaning is being reevaluated. Though Hispanic women may not be challenging the church very vocally, they are raising important questions through their praxis.

Hispanic women who are openly questioning their role in the church are not doing so without a tremendous amount of pain. It is extremely difficult for Hispanic women to risk alienation from the church because it is also risking alienation from the family and the culture, since these institutions are so tightly bound to each other. At the same time, many Hispanic women feel that the official church has abandoned them. Through its teachings and its documents, for example, it encourages them to take an active stance on behalf of justice, but it does not always support them when they do. Still other Hispanic women experience cognitive dissonance when they see the church calling other institutions to reform without reforming itself. The result is that there is an increasing number of Hispanic women having to struggle with the position that they will assume in relation to the official church. Most of these women do not want to leave the church but do not see how they can survive in it either.

A question that I have heard Hispanic women ask is, "How is this church going to understand what is happening to its people, if it will not listen?" In the case of Hispanic women, it is easier for church officials to continue to promote the stereotype of Hispanic women's traditional role in the church than to recognize the fact that many Hispanic women are leaving the church or, at best, relativizing it. Another fact that needs to be acknowledged is that Hispanic women are losing faith with the church for many of the same reasons as other women. As they develop a feminist consciousness, women find it difficult to remain in this institution and preserve integrity. A difference for Hispanic women is that we have consciously held on to tangible expressions of the faith within the lived experience of our family and community. This has helped us to preserve some semblance of relationship with the church and has encouraged our belief in the potential of the church to create community. In short, it is our faith and our religious imagination that have motivated our continuing in the church.

As Hispanic women we are aware that we have inherited a rich spiritual heritage. We are concerned about preserving it and we continue to draw strength from our foremothers' religious wisdom, but we are also conscious that their spirituality cannot completely satisfy us. Therefore, as we see the religious world of our mothers with all its devotions and rituals disappearing, we are challenged to identify the sources that will give us life. We know that the power that motivated our mothers and grandmothers was faith, not religion or church. It was their deep faith in God that sought nourishment in the church and in the community. It is the same faith in search of life that prompts many Hispanic women today to question their role in an institution that does not promote their growth or recognize their need. As they seek other ways to nurture their faith, Hispanic women are not only rediscovering community, they are "recreating" church.

EIGHT

Youth and Culture

Alicia C. Marill

ALICIA SANTANA, 20, IS A CUBAN RAISED IN MIAMI; JUAN, 18, IS A Chicagoan who has five sisters; Ana, 25, is from New Mexico and has a one-year-old son; Terry, 17, is Puerto Rican; Edgar, 17, is a Nicaraguan who has lived in California; Ilvis, 19, arrived from Cuba in 1980 with the group of refugees who left from the Mariel Harbor; Barbara, 18, is Cuban. Despite their varied backgrounds, they share a common experience: they are Hispanic youth living in the culture of the United States. Although at times they have felt caught between cultures, they have been able to "make peace" by observing the values of both worlds, affirming the good they see and rejoicing in their "double gift," as they call it. They talk about the values they saw in their parents' culture, the things they would change about it, the tensions they have experienced as they encountered a different culture, and the advice they would give to their parents and to their Hispanic young friends.

What values do you see in your culture?

Edgar: Religion is a very important value in our culture. My grandmother communicated that to me. It was nice to sit with her and pray; but not only that: I always saw in her a giving of herself; she was old when we came here, but since my parents had to work, she always walked us to school. She watched us and she loved it. She and my uncle taught me to give and to be grateful. These things have stayed with me as part of my life.

Ana: Hispanics are people of intense values. They are very willing to put themselves on the line for things that are important to them. We have a great sense of family and of tradition. There is a great pride in our roots, although sometimes it has been stifled by the dominant society through prejudice and discrimination.

Ilvis: Our people have a lot of courage; they have gone through terrible struggles and ordeals, but they survive and keep fighting.

Juan: There is a strong sense of togetherness. You graduate and you stay home. Unless there is a dire need to go someplace else because you need a job, the whole family stays in one place.

Terry: Hispanics have a great respect for education. Our parents instill in us a tremendous sense of respect for adults.

Is it all wonderful, or would you change something?

Alicia: Of course nothing is perfect! And sometimes, the same positive values we hold can be taken to extremes or distorted. Take, for instance, religion. Hispanics are very Catholic. This heritage is very strong. But we are very Catholic in a very traditional way; I mean, we go to church and that's it. We believe in the hierarchy, Sunday homilies, and so on, but whether or not we translate that into our own lives is another question.

Ana: What you say about religiosity also affects the way Hispanics view women. Women have traditionally been second-class citizens in the church. The Hispanic culture is very chauvinistic. I am not talking about an extreme, radical feminism but about the simple idea that a woman deserves as much as a man, and can be expected to live a full life; that she has as many options as a man has, as many capabilities, as much intelligence, and as much managerial experience as any man may have. That is hard to take for many Latin men.

Barbara: My parents will say things to me that will freak me out because I am a woman and because in their minds the role of a woman, her possibilities and her proper behavior, are distinctly different from those of a man. This puts as much of a strain on girls as on boys, who must act in a certain way or be considered gay, and really victimized.

Alicia: Another element I'd change is prejudice. Hispanics are ambitious people; they work very hard. But then, they don't understand why there is a homeless person living under a bridge when there is a job available at Burger King. People need to be taught to look at every aspect of their lives from a faith perspective. People tend to separate one thing from another. "I pray in the morning and before I go to bed, but that person on the street corner is not my problem." I think that attitude has to change.

Ilvis: There is a stereotype that Cubans who came after 1980 are all losers. I came in 1980, and I don't mean to sound conceited, but I get upset when I hear that, because when I look at my own life and the things I do, I know I am not a loser. The saddest part is that most of the discrimination these people receive is from other Cubans. When you are a minority, you try to step on whatever or whoever is lower. You need to be ahead of somebody else. I think that's what happened here.

Terry: Sometimes I find a certain intolerance among Hispanics. It makes me go insane to see somebody who left his or her country because there wasn't enough freedom or opportunity trying to shut up somebody else, trying to deny that person's right to think and act differently or to believe in certain things.

Barbara: I also see racism. My grandmother, for instance, would have a fit if I told her I have a black friend.

What has been most difficult for you to deal with?

Alicia: If I don't have a lot of problems with my parents, it is because I don't tell them every detail of what I do. A lot of times I keep things to myself. I do it because I know that my mother, for instance, would imagine things to be much worse than what actually happened. They are extremely protective, and even when I do good things, like getting involved in a homeless shelter, they worry about my safety.

Terry: Americans tend to bring up their kids to be independent. Hispanics teach them to be dependent. Many Hispanic parents do not see their child's individuality, and that's very important.

Ana: My parents have had their own share of conflicts when I started making decisions for myself. For instance, the first time I decided to take a trip there was a conflict.

Barbara: When I graduated from high school and wanted to go to the University of Florida, which isn't really that far from Miami, my parents had a fit. My grandparents live a block away from us because my mother has never been able to separate from them. For me this whole situation was a struggle; they laid a guilt trip on me, and I finally didn't go.

Juan: I grew up with five sisters, and I know the difference too. We are more protective of women. I can ask a woman out, and if she is an American, we just go out. But if she is Latin, I have to go and meet the whole family. My sister gets in the biggest fights with my mother because she lets me go out anytime, but my sister can't.

Terry: My Hispanic education totally avoided anything having to do with sexuality, so when I went to college I was totally unprepared for what I found; I had never heard the phrase "date rape," and I had no idea what that meant. Sending a girl out without a clue is more dangerous than sending her out alone if she has a notion of what to watch out for and how to protect herself. I would have found out ways of getting away from my brother watching over me, but I didn't have a clue of what to do to protect myself.

Edgar: Curfews are different for boys and girls. The father is very concerned for the security of his daughter. Preserving the decency of the family, "el honor de la familia," becomes an absolute, and that puts a lot of pressure on the girl.

Are Hispanic religious values ever at odds with the dominant culture?

Edgar: Living in the American culture for me sometimes has been a tension when I lost track of important values. I went to the Dominican Republic on a mission, and there we had nothing that we didn't absolutely need. But we had the people sharing with us, and we had a community. It is hard to see these values when you are surrounded by a culture that emphasizes consumerism and advertising. We start taking the easy, comfortable way out, and in the process we lose the sense of community.

The Latin culture is religion-oriented but it is harder to participate when you get here. There is a lot to take you away from religious feelings and practices. First of all, when you first arrive, you have a lot of worries which really are survival questions. Then, you have to confront consumerism. Young people first don't have the mental space necessary to think about religion; then, they find it is not acceptable within their peer group.

*If you could give some advice to your parents, and to the
parents of other Hispanic young people. . .*

Alicia: A lot of immigrant parents do not speak the language, don't know what's going on in the U.S. Life here is a lot more complicated than what it used to be. The kids go to school and come home and tell their parents what's going on. You are supposed to be their guide, and in an immigrant family that sometimes gets turned around and the kid becomes the guide for the parent. I find that situation dangerous. I think a lot is lost here in terms of the function of the family. I think this is one of the biggest problems of American society, because we have a big population of immigrants and this is a difficult situation for all of them. They switch roles; the parent's authority is undermined; they are no longer a role model for their kids. So I would tell them to try to educate themselves as soon as possible.

Ana: I'd say: if your kids are responsible and intelligent, and if you taught them well, let them go, let them live their lives. If you are confident that you brought them up right and the values that you instilled in them, and if you see in your daily life that you are living out those values, don't hold them back; let them leave.

Juan: Things have changed, so you have to move with the times.

Ilvis: I'd say two things:
    Don't think that your own experience is necessarily the same as your children's experience.
    If you are going to teach values, you have to be consistent. You cannot say prejudice is bad and then turn around and discriminate against those of your own people who came after you and who are not "the same." You can't say "be honest" and then find a wallet with $500 and all sorts of cards and keep it. You can't teach your children ambiguity because that's

teaching them to live in the most convenient way for themselves, not for others. If you are going to teach a child to be a Catholic, you have to act like a Catholic.

Edgar: Do not hold on to your own fears. Communicate more with your children to create trust.

Ana: Tell your kids that you are different and why. Be open to the possibility that your child is going to be different.

What would you tell Hispanic youth?

Ilvis: You should be proud of your heritage and your family. Don't turn away. Do not turn against other Hispanic groups that are not your own.

Barbara: Respect your parents and learn their history. Be aware that you don't have to be just Hispanic or just American; learn the values of both and keep what's good.

Ana: Recognize how much God has given us, because we have been gifted with two cultures, gifted with two experiences, and this should open the door to a new world for you; it should not close any doors. I have my own child now and I speak to him only in Spanish so that he doesn't lose his language, but I would hope that when he grows up, he'll learn about as many cultures as possible. I would hope to instill in him a tremendous pride in his roots.

Edgar: First, you have to be comfortable with yourself. You have to respect yourself, be confident of who you are, because otherwise, there will be mass confusion going on in your head. Sometimes I come across somebody who rejects his or her culture; and the reason is that other people hate the culture and so the person wants to fit in. These persons are not happy; in order to fit in, they have had to turn their backs on what they are. And when you don't know who you are, you cannot be happy.

NINE

Youth and Evangelization

Carmen María Cervantes

THE 500TH ANNIVERSARY OF THE COMING OF CHRISTIANITY TO America brought many controversies relevant to the evangelization of Latino youth in the United States. Today, just as 500 years ago, the mission to bring the Good News to young people and to incarnate the Gospel in their culture is marked by cultural shock and religious pluralism. Yet two differences exist. Half a millennium ago, the mission was to evangelize very religious people to whom Jesus was not known. Today, religious fervor is weak, but Latino youth are baptized and to some degree evangelized.

Reflecting on what happened five centuries ago can enlighten today's reality and identify appropriate paths for following Jesus and making his Reign vital to Latino youth. Some of the approaches and methods of evangelization used by the missionaries 500 years ago were an offshoot from the reality and experience of the native people, and were successful in delivering Christ and his message of salvation. Other approaches destroyed valuable elements of indigenous cultures and generated a religiosity in which the acceptance of the will of God led to passiveness in the face of exploitation and injustice. This history spurs some questions: What approaches and methods of evangelization are we using with our Latino youth? Are we conscious of the Latino cultural values that we want to preserve? Do we need to reinforce these values more? What approaches and methods of the American church do not fit in with the Latino *idiosincrasia* (the culture embedded in the personality of a particular ethnic group) and thus do not nurture our faith? What approaches do we need to develop further so that the evangelization of Latino youth will be more effective?

Evangelization and Culture

With rare exceptions, the Spanish missionaries did not differentiate between missionary and evangelization actions, colonial expansion, and cultural conquest. Evangelization presumes that the signs of the times are judged in light of the values of the Gospel and not those of the culture of the evangelizer. What perspective do we use when we analyze the life and values of Latino youth? What order of values do we promote when we seek their holistic development? Which ideals do we pursue in our ministry? What influences of the surroundings are more powerful than the Gospel?

Mestizo Identity

Latino youth in the United States are mestizos, with European and native or African blood. This biological and cultural mixture greatly influences the way they see themselves, understand their culture, and confront life. Therefore, we should reflect: How is it that as Latinos we are proud of our pre-Hispanic indigenous cultures, but we discriminate against and depreciate the native and poor people of our countries? Why is it so easy to recognize other nations or races as our oppressors and exploiters, but so difficult for us, when we reach positions of power and leadership, not to engage in the tyranny, abuse, and oppression of our own people? Why do we affirm our *mestizaje* but find it so difficult to assume the qualities, successes, errors, and failures of our various cultures of origin? How can we recognize and value our roots in order to promote ourselves as Latino-North American people? What does the process of Iberian-Latin American *mestizaje* teach us to confront in the new *mestizaje* in which we are involved? What can we do to face our prejudices and racism towards the African-American and Asian peoples and to overcome our feelings of inferiority in relation to the white society?

Pastoral Approach

For 500 years, the Latin American church has dedicated very few personnel and resources to evangelizing the indigenous and mestizo people in the rural areas and poor urban barrios, in comparison to the resources given to evangelizing the middle and upper classes in the cities. This has generated a classist church that leaves the majority of poor people with limited pastoral services. The Latin American Episcopal Conference, aware of Jesus' perspective on the poor, has tried to correct these mistakes from the past with its preferential option for the poor.

In the church in the United States, the *National Pastoral Plan for Hispanic Ministry* (1987) and the bishop's pastoral letter, *Justice for All: Social Teaching and the U.S. Economy* (1985), have also emphasized this option for the poor. Have we achieved consciousness and acceptance of this option throughout our North American church? What does this mean for the pastoral practice of our church and in our own ministry? How can we respond to the pastoral needs of Latino youth without isolating them from the mainstream North American church? How can we improve their catechetical formation so that they know, deepen, and mature in their faith?

Taking on the Past and Reconciling Ourselves

When analyzing a prior epoch, it is important to judge it with the criteria of that time and not with the mentality of the present era. At the same time, we should recognize and assume the mistakes, limited vision, and sins of the past with a spirit of reconciliation. This means that we should learn from history in order to review our own feelings, attitudes, and behaviors. We need to reconcile ourselves, asking for forgiveness of God and our brothers and sisters who have been hurt by the oppressions and injustices that originated in the encounter between the European and native cultures. Finally, we should commit ourselves to actively seeking the correction of the structural and social sins that have institutionalized oppression and injustice. We should ask ourselves: How can we balance the joy of evangelization with the sorrow and repentance for the damage done to so many people? How can we educate our youth and future generations so that the church and the multicultural society of the United States can live in harmony, valuing the differences of its members and working together for a better world? How can Christian Latino youth influence the adults in their family, school, and workplace in order to eradicate racism and structural injustice?

Today is the beginning of tomorrow. Latino youth, spreading their wings and taking off, are creating a better tomorrow. They are filled with challenges and hopes. To confront the challenges, they need a more profound evangelization and a holistic education. In the presence of hope, they need to keep flying higher and higher toward the endless possibilities that they have for growing as persons, promoting their own people, and following the way to God. This is the meaning behind the "New Evangelization" sought for by Pope John Paul II as the fruit of the Fifth Centenary of the Evangelization of America. This new evangelization should be—and already is—marked by new ardor, expressions, and methodologies that unfold in many Latino and Catholic youth groups and organizations.

New Ardor

The new ardor dwells in the sacredness and sanctity of life of our youth, in their prophetic and communitarian spirit, and in their consciousness that as youth they have a great stake in our future society and a mission to renew our church. This new ardor is also seen in young people's thirst to share their joy and gifts, in their process of growth and conversion, and in their apostolic enthusiasm to extend the Reign of God, mainly among other youth.

New Expressions

The new expressions are present in several dimensions of the life of young people. These expressions can be seen in their testimony of a life according to the values of the Gospel, searching to purify themselves and their modern culture of what is against the Reign of God. New expressions are also seen in young people's attempts to integrate a new Latino-North American culture with a set of values guided by those of Jesus, in their creation of new forms of popular religion that respond to their cultural reality and to the Christian vision of the world; and finally, in their growing commitment as a laity conscious of their mission in the world and in the church.

New Methodologies

In the last decade, new and more effective methods of evangelization took root in Hispanic youth ministry. The most prevalent may be the methodologies of Christian reflection based on a critical analysis in light of the Gospel and teachings of our church. Other methods help young people incarnate the message of the Gospel in their lives through a better comprehension of their personal development and of the cultural dynamic in which they are involved. In addition, there is the conviction that pastoral ministry should encourage a process of Christian *life,* not just programs, because pastoral ministry aims to further a pilgrim church traveling toward God. This young church forms prophetic, missionary, and evangelizing communities that provide a favorable environment for the human and Christian growth of the youth, who in turn are the salt, light, and yeast in the different environments in which they live.

Finally, young people realize more clearly day by day that without prayer and community life, the new methods do not facilitate the encounter with Jesus or the formation of young people as his disciples. Thus, the more mature youth groups are acquiring the characteristics of small communities. In these cases, the youth embrace a holistic evangelization approach that includes the methodological elements mentioned above entwined in an unbroken chain of critical analysis. Using Christian "eyes," the young people search for personal and community conversion, care for each other, work for the transformation of society and renewal of the church, celebrate their faith, and evaluate their Christian practice in the world.

Conclusion

Spreading their wings, Latino youth, supported by Hispanic youth ministry, are trying to confront the challenges that society, culture, and the church pose for them. They face the following challenges: a secularization that maintains a religious meaning of life and does not lose sight of the Christian values; a lack of testimony from Christians, which results in a need for serious efforts for a new evangelization; divisions within the church that call for a strong unity respecting the diversity of its members; the corruption of the social system; institutionalized injustices; and the loss of ethics and the lack of international solidarity that demand an open prophetism and effective transformative action. At the same time, these youth, convinced of their faith and proud Catholic tradition, strive for forming amiable and active communities that embrace and seek other Latino youth before they fall in the hands of atheism or have to search for God in other religious groups.

TEN

New Immigrants

Joseph P. Fitzpatrick

In THE EARLY HOURS OF SUNDAY MORNING, MARCH 25, 1990, A large number of Honduran immigrants were enjoying a weekend of fun together at the Happy Land social club, a hangout for Honduran soccer players, high school students and young folks in the Bronx. A Cuban who had been rejected from the club torched the main entrance. In the ensuing fire, 87 persons died, most of them Hondurans. It was a tragedy that shocked not only the nation of Honduras, where a day of national mourning was proclaimed; it shocked New Yorkers of all social levels who are hardened by the crime and the trials of life in the South Bronx.

But the ones on whom the tragedy fell like an unbearable burden were the Honduran immigrants themselves. To compound their grief was their isolation from one another. As *The New York Times* reported it, one of their greatest pains was that they had no place to grieve; no place to gather where they could feel *en su casa* (at home), a familiar spot where relatives and friends would meet, a tiny bit of turf in a large and complicated city that would be a little bit of home, of Tegucigalpa, or San Pedro Sula or La Ceiba; a place where they would know, without distraction, that they were still Hondurans, *El Pueblo de Honduras*. There was no political club, no large community center, no parish that would proclaim their identity, would tell the world who they were, most of all keep them aware of who they themselves were. They were scattered; they had to face the tragedy alone. Many generous priests, religious and lay people, especially at the local parish of St. Thomas Aquinas, were impressive in their support of religious faith and human compassion. But the care was as scattered as the Honduran people themselves.

This raises again, very sharply, the problem of the old national or language parish for newcomers to the city or nation. It raises again the importance of the close-knit, supporting system of the immigrant community that enabled earlier immigrants to New York to make it against impossible odds. The established citizens generally criticized the ghettos, the immigrant neighborhoods, the parishes where a foreign language was heard, where fiestas, celebrations, the important moments of baptism, marriage and burial moved with the same rhythms and the same style as in the old country. It was the immigrant community, bound together by the corner store, the home town club, the newspaper, the burial society, most of all the parish, the synagogue, the religious congregation. This was the source of stability and security, of mutual support and help—and sometimes exploitation—of the immigrants by their own. But it was "theirs," and it was this network of relatives and friends that gave the immigrants the strength to move with confidence and assurance into the mainstream of American life.

The Catholic Church met this challenge by the creative institution of the so-called national parish, the German parish, the Italian or Polish parish. This was the secure beachhead where the immigrants found priests, brothers, sisters and lay people speaking their own language, sensitive to the cultural background and style of the newcomers, recreating an environment where they were at home among their own, where they knew who they were and why they did the things that established residents found so strange. In the year 1902, apart from the English-speaking churches, the New York Archdiocese counted 13 German churches, two French, one Bohemian, four Polish, one Maronite, two Slovak, one Hungarian, one Spanish, 11 Italian and two for the blacks. There were many questions about these parishes: Would they divide the church, splinter it into ethnic groups, delay the learning of English and prevent the newcomers from becoming American? On the contrary, it was these very parishes at the heart of the immigrant community that gave the newcomers their sense of security in a strange land, that kept their sense of identity alive, that gave them the stability to "integrate from a position of strength" into American society.

However, the 1990s in New York CIty is not the 1890s. The city is different, the immigrants are different; even at its best, the experience of a modern newcomer has problems that previous immigrants never had to face. It is a crowded city now: eight million people is a far cry from four million. The pace of change is almost convulsive. Between 1970 and 1980, New York City lost 1,750,000 residents, descendents of the older European groups; they have gone to the suburbs. Meantime, there are two million Hispanics—Puerto Ricans, Cubans, Dominicans, Central and South Americans—taking their place. There are more than two million blacks, many from the Caribbean, others from the American South, an increasing number from Africa. Hundreds of thousands have come from Japan, China, Pakistan, India, Korea and the Philippines. New York has always been a city of newcomers, but never did it have such a variety in such numbers crowding into it in such a short time. The public schools have bilingual training in six or seven languages; they could never meet the language needs of all newcomers.

At the same time it is more difficult for immigrants to cluster as they once did. Affordable housing for poor people is a scarce commodity, and public housing Is governed by nondiscrimination policies. An immigrant cannot easily move into the same apartment where a brother, cousin or friend lives. The name is placed on a list, now thousands of names long; and selection is not only by turn, it is nondiscriminatory. It is true that, by reason of location, some projects are almost completely black or Hispanic. But the policy that seeks to protect each family's right to an equal chance becomes a barrier to the clustering of immigrants in the same house, apartment or block where friends or relatives live. And legalized status becomes another issue. If they are undocumented, they have a mountain of other problems: the Immigration and Naturalization Service announced that if any undocumented persons returned to Honduras for the burial of a family member, they would not be permitted to come back.

The parish, the heart of the community, has its own difficulties. Germans, Italians, Poles and others have moved to the suburbs; and the Archdiocese finds itself with large churches on its hands: German parishes with no Germans, Italian parishes with no Italians, Irish parishes with no Irish. When Hispanics arrive to take their place, the Archdiocese is not likely to start a Hispanic parish across the street from an almost empty German or Polish parish church. And there may be just enough of the old-timers around to make a fuss if their church is given to Hispanics or others. Where large concentrations of Puerto Ricans or Dominicans exist, this tends to take care of itself. But for people as scattered as the Hondurans, this is not so easy. Furthermore, there are few native Hispanic priests to accompany their people. For religious ministry, Hondurans, like other Hispanics, must often look to American priests who have learned Spanish and studied Hispanic cultures. Many of these priests are beloved by their Hispanic people, but it is not quite the same as the Irish with their Irish priest or the Germans with their German priest. And when the Hondurans find themselves in a Bronx, Manhattan or Brooklyn parish, they are most likely sharing the parish with Puerto Ricans, Dominicans, Cubans, Americans or Caribbean blacks. Thus the lament of the Hondurans: "We are all scattered; we have no place to grieve, where we can gather together and be at home."

Therefore, the central problem remains: How can the church minister to Hispanic people in the difficult circumstances described above, and fulfill the same function that the national parish fulfilled a century ago? This requires enormous creativity and effort. In some cases, a determined effort to create a sense of unity among the disparate groups of parishioners has been successful. I have seen some excellent examples of parishes where the efforts of a pastor or parish ministers or dedicated lay people have achieved a wonderful level of unity and collaboration. A sensitivity to the problem is essential to the deeply rooted need of immigrants to be able to create a satisfying community of their own, to whatever extent that is possible. Ministry in their own language and meaningfully related to their own culture is essential.

Urging them to learn English and adapt quickly to American ways is understandable among established residents, but this is not meeting the challenge. Hondurans, for example, will eventually learn English and adapt to American ways. All the immigrants have done so. But the immediate problem is to enable them to create a situation in which they have a sense of security among their own, the continuity of their way of life, a confidence in the sense of who they are. To achieve this in the turbulent variety of contemporary parishes, in the face of convulsive change, requires extraordinary effort. It is a challenge the church has never faced before. It must meet it now. It requires the courage to face the reality of the situation; the imaginativeness to innovate within older and out-of-date structures, and the willingness to face change. God gave the vision and courage to our predecessors of the last century. If we are responsive to God's call, we also may be blessed with the vision we need today to enable newcomers to create, in new and difficult situations, a satisfying sense of community; a basis of solidarity among their own, and a place, not only to grieve when tragedy occurs, but to grow as well as citizens of a new land.

ELEVEN

Empowering Leaders

Timothy M. Matovina

"WHEN ALL HAS BEEN SAID AND DUE DISCOUNT HAS BEEN MADE for the insufficiency of the data offered as the basis of a judgment, the conviction, we think, will cling to most readers' minds that there is an Italian problem, and that it clamors for solution . . ." ("The Italian Question," by the editors, *America*, 12/19/1914).

This statement came at the end of a two-month dispute in the pages of *America*, precipitated by the October 17, 1914, article, "Religious Conditions in Italy," by Joseph M. Sorrentino, S.J. Father Sorrentino's claim that the majority of Italians were "good practical Catholics" incited a flurry of letters to the editor arguing the existence of a "problem" in Italian religious practice. Although his essay focused on religious practice in Italy, his respondents debated the religiosity of Italian immigrants in the United States as well. Their comments reveal parallels between accusations leveled at Italian immigrants of that time and today's Hispanic Catholics, and between the response of the church in the United States to each.

The accusations directed at Italians in the *America* correspondence included charges of false piety and emotionalism in their public processions and popular devotions. Italian Catholics were also characterized as ignorant of their faith, infrequent in church attendance and unwilling to offer support (financial or otherwise) to parishes. For these reasons they were deemed easy targets for Protestant proselytizing efforts. Their defenders in the letter exchange questioned the legitimacy of the so-called Italian problem and considered it the product of the hostility these immigrants so frequently met in the United States, even from members of their own church.

The final letter before the editor closed the controversy hinted at the most effective response made by the U.S. church to the Italian "problem." To the extent that the Italian situation was addressed successfully, it was addressed by the promotion of leadership for Italian faith communities, particularly the leaders who came from the Italian community itself, *e.g.,* the Scalabrinians, St. Frances Xavier Cabrini's Missionary Sisters of the Sacred Heart, and Italian diocesan clergy. The emergence of this indigenous leadership enabled other concerns also to be addressed, *e.g.,* participation in parish life, outreach to the unchurched and cultural sensitivity in ministry.

The U.S. hierarchy has not spoken of a Hispanic "problem" but has gone on record as seeing the Hispanic community as "a blessing from God" and "a unique pastoral opportunity" (*The Hispanic Presence: Challenge and Commitment,* 1983). Despite this official declaration, however, misunderstanding and unwarranted criticism of Hispanic religious practice and participation in church life have not been eliminated. Although not as public as the criticism of Italian Catholics in the pages of *America* 80 years ago, the lack of cultural sensitivity evidenced in much of this criticism damages Hispanic faith communities. Even when sensitivity to Hispanic religion and culture is attempted by bishops, pastors and others, there is continuing frustration at the tremendous need and scarcity of personnel and resources for Hispanic ministry. The seeming immensity of any proposed undertaking often leads to paralysis in our ministry with Hispanics.

A possible antidote for cultural insensitivity and for this paralysis is to employ the strategy found most effective in responding to the Italian "problem," *i.e.,* the formation of indigenous leadership. Leadership formation is one of the four specific dimensions of the U.S. bishops' *National Pastoral Plan for Hispanic Ministry* (1987). The Italian immigrant experience suggests that promoting indigenous leadership will stimulate a domino effect with regard to other concerns for Hispanic ministry, *e.g.,* the sounder pastoral planning, evangelization and missionary outreach also called for in the *National Pastoral Plan.* That leadership formation is the best starting point for Hispanic ministry today is confirmed by the recent national survey on Hispanic ministry conducted by the National Conference of Catholic Bishops and the U.S. Catholic Conference Secretariat for Hispanic Affairs, in which dioceses surveyed report that lay leadership formation programs have been the most helpful aspect of the *Plan*.

How can we operate in such a way that our pool of Hispanic ministers steadily increases? One way is to prioritize funding for efforts that are successfully fostering Hispanic leadership, *e.g.*, centers like the Mexican American Cultural Center in San Antonio, Texas, and the community organizing projects supported by the Campaign for Human Development. Another way is to evaluate diocesan and parochial ministerial activity by asking, "How will this activity enable more effective leadership to emerge for Hispanic ministry?" To cite one example, a program for baptismal preparation would be deemed most effective if it not only provided adequate catechesis, but also identified, called forth and trained new leaders to assist in giving that catechesis. The formation of leaders cannot be limited to liturgical ministries, however, nor can it be confined to an "old guard" or some other elite group. Often leaders do not come forth until personally invited by diocesan personnel, pastors or other church staff members. Discussion of whom to invite for specific ministries should be a consistent agenda item for staff and pastoral planning meetings.

Community organizers have speculated that pastors typically dedicate 90% of their time to dealing with people's personal problems and 10% to the formation of committed parishioners for ecclesial ministries. The primary challenge facing Hispanic (and other) pastoral agents today is how to reverse this trend, utilizing the bulk of our time, energy and financial resources for the formation of indigenous leaders who are the lifeblood of local communities.

In an age of tight budgets, hectic schedules and multiple needs, choosing leadership formation as a starting point is an effective way to promote ministry with our Hispanic sisters and brothers. Our tradition as a church of Italian and other immigrants is a valuable resource in this effort; that tradition impels us to see the Hispanic presence as an opportunity to enrich the church with an untapped wealth of leadership.

TWELVE

Formation in Religious Communities

Verónica Méndez

IN THE APRIL 9, 1990 ISSUE OF *TIME*, THE COVER STORY, "BEYOND the Melting Pot," reports that early in the 21st century racial and ethnic groups in the United States will outnumber non-Hispanic whites for the first time. The largest number of Catholics in this new "majority" are Hispanics. Already one-fourth of the U.S. people define themselves as Hispanic ("Hispanic" is being used here to refer to all people who are the result of the miscegenation of Spanish, indigenous and African. It is an adequate term, but there is no one term satisfactory to everyone). With an estimated future growth of 21%, this number is not likely to drop. The actual figures, however, though impressive in themselves, do not tell the whole story. In reality, due to conditions such as the lack of legal documents, poverty, low education and more, Hispanics are hard to count and an official census misses a good number of them.

It Used to be Easier

No one denies the impact Vatican II has had on the church throughout the world. Few took to heart the call for renewal and adaptation as seriously and completely as the communities of women religious in the United States.

This rapid renewal has resulted in the ongoing identity crisis that most communities in this country have been going through since the latter half of the 1960s. Many credit this lack of a clear identity as one of the major reasons for the diminishing numbers in religious communities. In an article in *America* (10/24/92), Dennis Castillo gives us yet another reason. He points out that the origin of the priest and religious shortage really began in 1942! Presently, we have a greater ratio of priests to Catholics in the United States than we had then. This article also points out that the number of men and women joining priesthood and religious life begins to drop when the immigration generation starts to join the mainstream of U.S. Catholics. As we will see later on in this article, this is true for Hispanics also. The highest level of interest in priesthood and religious life is among the newly arrived immigrants. But they are the ones who have the most obstacles in this journey. In many ways the changes following Vatican II have made it more difficult for Hispanics to be attracted to religious life and to stay if they choose to join. In some ways, before Vatican II, the process of integration was easier because, though Hispanics may have been joining communities whose dominant culture was different than their own, they were joining communities which also had a certain religious subculture that gave those communities their identity and those joining something to begin to identify with. The Hispanics who joined religious life in the 1950s or early 1960s found a group of people who dressed alike (habit), followed the same schedule (horarium), participated in the same apostolates, prayed in the same manner, recreated at the same time, ate the same food.

Today, Hispanics who join religious communities in the United States find that these communities are definitely American, that English is a "sine qua non" for membership, and that before they can vest themselves with the charism of the community, they must first don the U.S. culture of its members. Could this be one of the main reasons why Hispanics, and the poor in general, do not stay in religious life? The matter of culture is so important that even Hispanic Americans born in the United States who speak English have found it difficult to remain in U.S. religious communities.

La Realidad

Doing a socio-historical analysis of the reality of Hispanics and comparing it with that of United States religious communities should shed some light on why so few Hispanics stay in their congregations. In this section we will look at several aspects of this reality: differences in culture, acculturation, economic reality, education, church, vocations, Catholic practice and spirituality.

Culture

The recent commemoration of the Quincentennial has helped to highlight the genuine *mestizaje* of Hispanic cultures. Our indigenous, Iberian and African roots make us the people we are today. This miscegenation is part of what contributes to the plurality which exists among Hispanic Americans.

Hispanics across this country have much in common and much that differentiates them. They share a common language and values. They also share a common faith. However, though they share many of the same cultural values (family, hospitality, religiosity, and such), they do not have a common culture. One of the reasons "Hispanic" is such an inadequate term is that it refers to a population that comes from 21 different countries with 21 different histories and cultures! This is one of the reasons it is so difficult to find one word that adequately describes this reality.

Around 75% of Hispanics still identify themselves as Catholic, and the greater majority of them express this faith through their popular religion. They also share a common youthfulness. The median age of Hispanics is 22; twice as many Hispanics are under 18 years of age than in the total population. Mexicans are the youngest of this group. When this reality is compared with that of U.S. religious communities, we find that most of their membership have their cultural roots in Europe, many in northern Europe. The ambience in many of these communities is more monocultural than culturally pluralistic. Moreover, the culture that dominates is not European, but rather that of white middle-class United States. The language shared is English and the race tends to be white.

Another component of their reality which must be looked at is the different styles of community living presently experienced by many religious. As anyone who works with Hispanics knows, community is a very high value for them. Today, however, it becomes more and more common to find religious living alone and sometimes geographically far from their communities. We in religious life are still trying to define what community means to us. How do we explain that to a young person whose culture is steeped in very deep communitarian roots?

The age factor also comes into play here. Due to the lack of recent vocations, the median age of the U.S. religious is on the rise. How do we go about inviting these young Hispanics into aging communities? More to the point, how do we form them?

Levels of Acculturation

Acculturation here is being understood as denoting the level of influence the dominant culture of this country has on the culture of the Hispanics who live here. From this standpoint, Hispanics in this country are many people: some were here over 100 years before the arrival of the English, some were born here of immigrant parents, others were born in their Hispanic country but raised here, and still others are newly arrived. Some of these Hispanics speak only English, some speak both English and Spanish; for some, English is their predominant tongue, for others Spanish predominates. The greater number of newly arrived speak only Spanish.

Perhaps because the newly arrived are more noticeable—they do not blend in as well with the rest of the population—there is a tendency to think they are the majority. In actuality, only 30% of Hispanics are newly arrived; 70% were either born or raised here. Nearly one-half of the Hispanics who answered the 1990 census claimed English as their first language. Even the church errs here: 70% of the church's efforts with Hispanics are spent on the 30% of newly arrived.

Again, the experience of U.S. religious is different. The majority of their ancestors did not immigrate from Latin American countries. And, though the melting pot theory is no longer the mentality of all U.S. religious, many still hold onto it. Hispanics, however, tenaciously hold on to not only being Hispanic but specifically being Mexican, Puerto Rican, Cuban, Nicaraguan, or other.

The Church

The immigrant church that the ancestors of the U.S. religious experienced was also different from the one Hispanic people find. One big difference is that the European Catholic who immigrated to this country arrived here with their priests and religious to serve them. As Joseph Fitzpatrick, S.J., notes, it was this group of feisty immigrant priests and sisters who fought for the rights of the different ethnic groups they represented. National churches were formed for Italians, Germans and Poles, leaving the other parish de facto the Irish national church. It was from these national churches that the different immigrant groups moved into the mainstream of the United States, Catholic and secular, and they could do so precisely because the church had provided for them a space where their ethnic identity was affirmed instead of threatened. These national parishes gave these immigrants time to move from their first ethnic identity to whatever level of American acculturation they chose. But the Hispanic immigrants arrive here without their priests or religious. The reason for this is very simple: they do not have them. The history of the church in Latin America is not one in which native vocations were encouraged by the official church. From its earliest days the efforts of the missionaries to produce native vocations was at best apathetic and at worst laced with racism.

Even the church the Hispanic immigrant finds is different from that of the ancestors of U.S. religious. Though the history and growth of the U.S. Catholic Church can only be understood in terms of its multi-ethnic heritage, the Hispanic Catholic finds that this post-immigrant church is one in which: ". . . its ethnic memory is fading and its agenda articulates well national concerns of egalitarianism, democracy, individualism, women's rights." (Fr. Tomasi, "The Pastoral Challenges of the New Immigration." June 1989. FADICA. Washington, D.C.)

Women's rights is one of the social justice issues which the women of the U.S. Catholic Church attempt to keep on the agenda of the U.S. hierarchy. However, it is very difficult for Hispanic (and black) women, the majority of whom are poor and not highly educated, to identify and own the movement as it is presented by white, non-Hispanic, middle-class women.

Economics and Education

The lifestyle of the greater number of U.S. religious communities is that of middle or upper-middle class America. Priests and religious are among the best educated in the United States. On the other hand, over 60% of Hispanics drop out of high school. Among Puerto Ricans, the number will often be as high as 70%. Economically, though there does exist a small number of middle-class Hispanics and even a smaller number of wealthy ones, Hispanics are mostly working-poor, marginal, with many below the poverty line. 38% of all Puerto Rican families in the United States were living in poverty in 1987; 30% blacks; 26% for all Hispanics; 10% for white, non-Hispanics.

Vocations

There is no question that Hispanics are disproportionately under-represented among clergy and religious. Proportionate to their number in the 1980s, there should have been at least 17,000 priests. Instead there were only 1,400 and only about 180 of these were born in this country. The same disparity applies to Sisters and Brothers. Later figures are not much better. A 1989 CARA report shows the small number of Hispanics who reach first vows: 7% of those join mixed clerical institutes, 4% join Brothers' communities, and 9% join Sisters' communities. Vocational work with Hispanics has shown that the newly arrived Hispanic youth is much more interested in the possibility of religious life than the U.S. Hispanic. Among these latter, vocation interest is no higher than it is with the rest of U.S. youth. However, *the newly arrived Hispanic is the least acceptable to U.S. communities and, though the Hispanic Americans might be acceptable, it is questionable whether they have really been courted.*

It might be appropriate to discuss here the question of standards for acceptance into our seminaries and religious communities. In his article "The Vocation Crisis" (Paulist Press, 1989), Howard Gray, S.J., writes that today we continue to look for qualified women and men. "Consequently, our first future direction should be to continue to articulate our understanding of our problems and to resist meeting these by lowering our admittance standards."

I have often heard this said and have insisted upon it myself for fear that we may be perceived as thinking that Hispanics cannot meet our high standards. Lately, however, I have begun to question the standards. *Who decides them? On which set of values are they based?* In this country there is a double standard for the English- and Spanish-speaking candidates for priesthood. Here a young man cannot enter a seminary or be ordained unless he can master English well enough to do work at a philosophical and theological level. By contrast, even though the Church he is going to serve is almost 50% Hispanic, an English-speaking person will be ordained whether or not he speaks Spanish. While some dioceses make the ability to say Mass and hear confessions in Spanish a requirement for ordination, they do not require that the candidate do his M.Div. studies in Spanish. The same leeway is rarely given to the person who perhaps masters English well enough to say Mass and hear confessions but would need to do their studies in Spanish.

The equivalent of this double standard for women is that many United States communities require college completion or some years in college before entrance. In some communities, the candidate who enters without a mastery of English is sometimes held back from novitiate or vows until she acquires a proficiency in the language that satisfies the community. I bring up these questions because I ask myself, *why do we accept Hispanic candidates in the first place? Whom do we prepare them to serve?* One of the big problems in formation is that by the time we finish forming our Hispanic candidates, they are so alienated from the communities they come from that they no longer want to return to them. Another question I ask myself is, *can we really say that our people are not ready for ministry unless they are highly educated? Is it possible that those who may not be able to do advanced education in this country might still be very well-equipped to serve a people they know well?* Virgilio Elizondo likes to tell the story of a young man in his parish who evangelizes among the youth and drug addicts. He does not have much education and cannot speak English well, but he is one of the best evangelizers Elizondo has met.

Religious Practice

The Hispanic who comes to our religious communities often has a spirituality and practice far more akin to popular religion than to that which is understood by the term "practicing Catholics." It is possible that this young person comes from a family that is deeply religious and prayerful but perhaps is not at Sunday Mass too often. In contrast, the majority of our religious communities have their spiritual roots in the same Europe their ancestors came from and many of our members were blessed with practicing Catholic families.

The Sisters in my Catholic grammar school gave such wonderful impressions of those Catholic homes they came from that I arrived at the conclusion that no community would ever accept me because few in my family ever went to Mass!

Towards an Inculturated Model of Formation

The formation of an Hispanic and the successful evangelization of a different culture have much in common. Inculturation is a word increasingly used by theologians to express the relationship between the Christian message/life and cultures. It speaks of a relationship between faith and culture that is true to both faith and culture. It is, then, an active process of insertion of the faith into the culture.

Religious Life and Inculturation

Almost everything I say about religious life and inculturation is due to Marcello de C. Azevedo who, in an article he wrote (*"Evangelization-Inculturation-Religious Life: Principles and Criteria,"* IUSG no. 77, 1988), applies the principles of inculturating the evangelical message to the various charisms in religious life. It has slowly dawned on us that for the past five centuries the church has spread the gospel in Latin America principally, and almost exclusively, through the traditional, European, especially Mediterranean culture. Religious institutes were effective instruments of the transmission and construction of this ecclesial uniformity. As they planted religious life in our midst, especially the international congregations and orders, they followed, in principle, the same model. The vision of the Gospel and of the religious charism maintained both in the congregation and in the new world were strongly subordinated to the point of view of the institute's context of origin or of that predominant in it. There resulted uniformity in almost everything: language, dress, the methods and criteria of judging and action and the formation of individuals, which became the same here as in the place of origin of the institute. Today, however, the process of opening up to the apostolic need of inculturating the Gospel message has led many congregations also to the inculturation of religious life itself.

Principles, Aspects of Inculturation

With very few exceptions, the evangelization that has been carried out throughout the centuries has not been concerned much with the inculturation of the faith. Likewise, the price of *La Conquista* and the evangelization that followed was the destruction of the preexisting cultures and a lack of respect for them. Karl Rahner notes this historical reality: despite the implied contraction to its essence, the actual concrete activity of the church in its relation to the world outside of Europe was in fact (if you will pardon the expression) the activity of an export firm which exported a European religion as a commodity it did not really want to change but sent throughout the world together with the rest of the culture and civilization it considered superior ("Towards a Fundamental Theological Interpretation of Vatican II," *Theological Studies,* December 1979).

The resulting culture, still felt today, is manifested in the dependency, faulty tendency to imitate, inferiority and insecurity found in most Latin American and other Third World countries.

Today there is a basic assumption that there can be no complete evangelization without true inculturation. We have come to realize that the Christian message can be lived in and by any culture without destroying either the message or the culture.

Application to Religious Life

Much of what has been said above can be applied to the formation of an Hispanic in a U.S. community. If it is our desire not to cause more culture ruptures in our attempts to integrate others into our religious communities, then we must try to apply these principles of inculturation to our formation programs. The formation program can begin, as the theological process does, with the opening of culture, that long and careful listening to a culture to discover its principal values, needs, interests, directions and symbols. Needless to say, this kind of listening must be done by the formation person and the one being formed.

Model of Inculturation of the Faith

The model of inculturation given to us by Marcello Azevedo, S.J., (IUSG, 1988) is represented in four stages that, though analytically distinct, can unfold in an integrated manner and even simultaneously. These four stages are:

1. *The anthropological-theological identification of the culture.* That is, one should get to know the culture one is attempting to evangelize.

2. *Recognizing the limits inherent in the culture.* Since no culture is absolute and each shares in the sinfulness, frailty and lack of harmony of the rest of humanity, in this stage one tries to identify those things that are incompatible with the Gospel.

3. *The explicit proclamation of the Gospel.* This would be something new in relation to the culture. This is, of course, the proclamation of the gift that comes to us in Jesus Christ.

4. *This announcement is made by and from within a community which accepts the Gospel and tries to live and spread it, the church.*

The result of this process in time is but an expression of the faith by a different culture in its own way. The expression will have a specific identity since it comes from specific roots. But it will also have a found unity inasmuch as these cultural ecclesial communities are inspired by the same faith, which is the source and incentive of communion. This unity is built on the conscious diversity of culture rather than on uniformity. It eliminates the imposition of one culture on another as the exclusive mediator of the faith.

An Inculturated Model of Formation

We will begin by using Azevedo's descriptions of inculturation and paraphrasing them to apply to formation instead of evangelization. Inculturation is the process of formation by means of which the charism of the community is inserted gradually into the culture of the candidate. It is the process of formation by which the seed of the charism is cast into the soil of the candidate's culture. The germ of the charism then develops in the terms and according to the particular genus of that culture which receives it. Inculturation is the process of formation by which the community life and message are assimilated by the candidate's own cultural style in such a way that they not only are expressed by means of the elements proper to the culture, but also constitute a principle of inspiration as well as a norm and power of unification which transforms, recreates and projects this culture.

Relying on the above, then, we would describe the four stages of the formation program in this manner.

1. *The anthropological-theological identification of the culture of the candidate.* That is, one should ask questions that would give one information on the reality the candidate is coming from.

2. *Recognizing the limits inherent in the candidate's culture.* What in it is incompatible with the Gospel and, therefore, also incompatible with the community's charism? It is the incompatibility with the Gospel that is important here. It does not necessarily apply that because some element of the candidate's culture is incompatible with the dominant culture of the community it is also incompatible with that community's charism!

3. *The explicit proclamation of the community's charism.* This is what the community can offer to the candidates which would be new to them and their culture and reaches beyond both of these. This gift is offered in the same way the gift of Jesus Christ is offered. It does not need to disfigure nor do violence to the candidate's culture. Rather, this gift should be one more means by which one can rise to the fullness of one's human, individual and social potentiality.

4. *This announcement is made by, from and within the community the candidate has joined,* a community which accepts the Gospel and tries to live it, a community which is part of the church.

Difficulties

U.S. religious communities, being as much the products of our time as anyone else, also have some distance to go before an inculturated formation program is a reality in our different communities. The radical change of attitude that is needed in our church is needed in our religious communities also. This, of course, means that we have to learn to let go, something we all find very difficult. But if the church has to drop its traditional defensive posture before inculturation becomes a reality, then religious communities also have to drop their defenses before multicultural religious communities can become a reality in the United States.

Despite the difficulty, I am convinced that none of our communities can afford to escape this new process of change. Today, in many of our congregations, we often discuss the prospect of our death as religious communities. The age of our Sisters and the lack of vocations make this a very real possibility. Though many communities are experimenting with alternate styles of membership, the reality of approaching death remains imminent for a number of our communities. Another frequent topic in religious communities today is that of refounding. I think it can be said that all our communities were founded by people who had marvelous vision and an accurate sense of what their times needed. Many who continue to believe in the future of religious life also believe that we will manage to survive only if we can respond to the needs of our times with the same accuracy that our founders did.

THIRTEEN

Catechesis

Angela Erevia

WHAT CAN WE CATECHISTS LEARN FROM OUR HISPANIC BROTHERS and sisters? How do we deal with their presence in our communities? What should we be doing to assist them to be *at home* in our church groups? How can we more effectively reach Hispanic children and youth? And finally, what can we learn from the way Jesus approached people?

Our principal mission as catechists is to lead children to Jesus: to help them discover the "Jesus" in themselves and in others. Scripture tells us how Jesus did this. "Some people brought children to Jesus for him to touch them, but the disciples scolded those people. When Jesus noticed it, he was angry and said to his disciples, 'Let the children come to me, and do not stop them, because the Kingdom of God belongs to such as these. Remember this! Whoever does not receive the Kingdom of God like a child will never enter it.' Then he took the children in his arms, placed his hands on each of them, and blessed them" (Mark 10:13-16).

We can lead Hispanic children to Jesus effectively only when we assure them that Jesus blesses them, too, *just as they are*. They have great value in his eyes. Their cultural background, family systems, language, religious expressions, and cultural traditions are all loved and blessed by Jesus. As proclaimers of Jesus, we have to make a sincere effort to learn all we can about our Hispanic sisters and brothers.

What Should We Know?

Hispanic families are a very intricate system: father, mother, brothers, sisters, aunts, uncles, cousins, and all the in-laws. In addition, there are *los hijos de crianza* (children brought up by parents other than the biological parents), *los tocayos* (namesakes), *madrinas y padrinos* (godmothers and godfathers), *compadres y comadres* (a spiritual bond created between parents and godparents), and *amigos and amigas* (friends).

A child's birth is a blessing. The expression *criatura de Dios* (literally "creature of God" but meaning "child of God") is always used with a deep sense of love and gratitude to God when addressing or speaking to a child or adult. Birthdays always call for a fiesta. Fiestas celebrate life by celebrating the God of the fiesta, the giver of life!

Hispanics clearly and firmly believe that God is creator and Father of all, and life is a gift from God. With this gift they receive their parents, race, culture, and a particular historical setting. They believe one should go through life celebrating the gift of who they are. Their dignity is based on being created in the image of God, and reverence and respect are due to all God's children. They accept cultural differences and celebrate them as God's gift. They use art, music, and dance to celebrate their cultural and historical events.

The Home Is Central

For Hispanic children, as for all children, the family is either a source of identity and security or a source of fragmentation and violence. The home, the domestic church, is the primary place where children experience God. They experience God in the beauty of family life with all its expressions of love, care, security, and gratitude. Through visual images, the Hispanic child very early in life learns that "God is love."

They sometimes learn, too, that the full expression of God's love is Jesus' death on the cross. Suffering can often be a normal part of life. Thus the crucifix is their primary symbol of God's love and forgiveness. In difficult moments like death, Hispanic adults constantly invoke God in explaining death to their children. "So and so is in heaven with God" is the usual expression.

The home is also the place where Hispanic children learn the reality of sin and its devastating effects, especially on family life. They are taught to recognize sin in the harsh expressions of hatred, grudges, and revenge. Catechists are influential persons who can assist these children to make sense of their reality. By acknowledging that for Hispanic children both good and evil are centered around family life, catechists can help them affirm their family traditions and uphold the religious reality of being a *criatura de Dios*.

Ways to Celebrate

Catechists should celebrate this "child of God" reality with occasional class fiestas, community-oriented celebrations that reinforce family relationships. For Hispanic children, the piñata is part of fiesta. Created by the Augustinians, the piñata was a creative way to evangelize the indigenous peoples of Mexico. It was originally made in the form of the devil to symbolize sin and evil in the human condition.

The blindfold, worn by the ones trying to break the piñata open, symbolized the human tendency to be "blind" to sin and evil. The stick, used for breaking the piñata, symbolized the rod of Christian virtue. Several persons hitting the piñata symbolized the community needed to "break" evil. Once the piñata is broken, goodies fall to the ground, symbolizing the blessing of God on the entire community.

Following are some additional activities you may want to incorporate into your classes with Hispanic children.

- *Celebrate class aniversarios* (anniversaries) of baptism and other significant religious events.

- Identify music, art, poems, and stories about Hispanics and use them as examples in your lessons.

- Use the *piñata* at celebrations and explain its significance.

- Sponsor an annual Mass for all 15-year-olds for their *quince años,* explaining the tradition.

- Reflect on death customs, including the *velorio* (wake service), *Misa* (Mass of the Resurrection), *entierro* (burial), *novenario* (nine days of prayer after the burial).

Since Advent provides opportunities for drama, bright colors, art, music, and danza (ritual dance), consider these suggestions.

- Dramatize the story of Our Lady of Guadalupe, particularly Our Lady's message to Blessed Juan Diego.

- Dramatize Joseph and Mary looking for shelter in Bethlehem and the birth of Jesus (the custom of *las posadas*).

- Use the piñata at celebrations, explaining its significance before it is broken open.

FOURTEEN

The Challenge of Proselytism

J. Juan Díaz Vilar

WILL THE LATIN PEOPLE WHO LIVE IN THE UNITED STATES CON-
tinue to be Catholics in the future? What is the reason for the
success of the sects among the Latin people? Are the sects a
threat to the Catholic Church? What's to be done about the
challenge of the sects and new religious movements? These and
many more questions frequently emerge in publications and pastoral meetings, as well as in the ecclesiastic environment and the
media.

The Expansion of the Sects

The phenomenon of the sects has always been present
throughout the history of Christianity and other religions. These
past few years have seen the strongest and most successful expansion of the sects. For a time many people thought that this
phenomenon was simply a fanatic fever and that it would pass,
but it has not. Today the mainline churches consider the sects to
be a very serious problem. One recent survey found that each
year in the United States 100,000 Latins leave the Catholic
Church to join a sect!

The Vatican document titled *Report on Sects, Cults and
New Religious Movements* tells us that the most vulnerable
groups in the church, especially the youth, seem to be the most
affected—especially when they are "footloose," unemployed, not
active in parish life or voluntary parish work, come from an un-
stable family background or belong to ethnic minority groups.

The Power of the Sects

We may ask ourselves why people decide to join the sects, why these new religions attract such a large following, or why they have such success with the youth.

From a general perspective it can be said that the success of the sects comes mainly because of two factors:

1. Their constant activity. Because they are well-programmed and well-funded, they are able to reach their goals. Their proselytizing activity is intense through home visits and invitations offered on the streets and in the work places, as well as through the media.

2. Their seeming ability to fill a need. Many Hispanics experience pastoral emptiness and an identity crisis in the Catholic parishes. This is what the sects and cults try to remedy, and to quite an extent they are succeeding.

In my book, *Las Sectas, un desafío a la pastoral* (New York: Northeast Catholic Pastoral Center for Hispanics), I list what I believe are the 10 most significant reasons for the success of the sects and cults:

1. They make good use of the media.

2. They offer membership in small communities.

3. They help their members to escape from anonymity.

4. They provide for everyone's active participation in the church.

5. They provide a mystique, a spirituality and a commitment.

6. They have a simple doctrine and a good catechesis.

7. They stress the Bible and preaching.

8. They instill a vision of hope.

9. They give their members a cultural identity.

10. They have clear strategies.

I will reflect below on the last two reasons I listed for the Pentecostals' success with Hispanics.

Strategy Planning

Each group has its own method of proselytizing, but we can say that *all the sects have a pastoral plan for Hispanics that has concrete strategies and goals* which are brought into practice with precision and an abundance of means.

One of the best organized activities of the sects, and the most efficient, is the pastoral invitation to assist in the local church and later to join the sect. For many sects the visits to homes is their most important activity. It is easy to believe that all those people that visit homes and preach in the streets are simply fanatics to whom we should pay no attention. This opinion is false. The reality is that the sects carefully prepare their aggressive strategies with methods that are practical, concrete, and easily evaluated. These home visits are not simply out of courtesy, or to take a survey. When they go, they offer something—something very attractive to many. Among the things they offer are simple and clear answers, an unabashed religious fervor, and community.

Let's take a look at an example of some of the Pentecostal strategies.

1. The Pentecostals organize Bible classes where they implant the idea that God and the Bible are, after all, the same in every church. They frequently make statements like, "Come to my church—you can learn about God in any place."

2. Many Hispanic people, hungry for good preaching and biblical knowledge, go not with the idea of changing their religion, but to share God's Word, something that they have not always found easy in their own church.

3. Once the Hispanics go to Pentecostal classes, they are told that idolatry is being practiced in their own church—and that adoration of the Virgin and the

saints is prohibited by the Bible. The sacraments are questioned and criticized as well.

4. The criticism of the Catholic faith becomes more tolerable to the Hispanics because of the environment of friendship and love provided by the Pentecostals. When one goes inside a Pentecostal church, from the beginning he or she is greeted and welcomed as someone special and given a great deal of attention. All the church members pray for his or her problems and for conversion.

We live in a cold world—a place where interpersonal relations are more and more difficult to establish. For immigrants, loneliness and a lack of identity can increase at an alarming pace.

This coldness is felt especially by the Latin immigrant who comes from a culture which is more given to expression, openness and warm communication.

With the Pentecostals, Hispanics find this human warmth. They are strongly attracted to the friendship found in a small Christian community—the feeling of family. This helps them to overcome the problem of anonymity and loneliness.

The Chilean sociologist, Carmen Galilea, became a part of the Pentecostal world for six months in order to study it from the inside. She found the following:

"Being in a Pentecostal cult is like participating in a large family. One finds herself in her own home, where feelings and emotions are expressed—a place that lacks formality and is full of human warmth." (Los Pentecostales: Elementos para una reflexión pastoral. Santiago de Chile, 1990).

The small communities organized by Pentecostals facilitate personal contact and friendship. In these types of communities a lonely person can find his or her identity, and friends—and in a very deep way live free from anonymity.

The Vatican document I referred to earlier has this to say about this aspect of why the small communities succeed:

People feel a need to rise out of anonymity, to build an identity, to feel that they are in some way special and not just a number or a faceless member of a crowd. Large parishes and congregations, administration-oriented concern and clericalism, leave little room for approaching every person individually and in the person's life situation. (1.1.5)

In addition to this freedom from anonymity, they offer participation in the tasks and ministries which provide a sense of belonging, of identity. They and the church are one and the same. Quoting again from the Vatican document:

The sects appear to offer: human warmth, care and support in small and close-knit communities; protection and security, especially in crisis situations; resocialization of marginalized individuals (for instance, the divorced or immigrants); the sect often does the thinking for the individual. (2.1.1)

And with reference to the Catholic Church it states:

The church is often seen simply as an institution, perhaps because it gives too much importance to structures and not enough to drawing people to God in Christ. (5.2)

A study published by the National Catholic Educational Association expresses it this way:

Hispanics in the church today have testified that they do not feel accepted by the church. They do not experience acceptance of their culture, their language, and their popular expressions of religion. Testimony indicated that large numbers of Hispanics are finding the acceptance they seek in fundamentalist churches. These religions are using their resources to provide Hispanics with Spanish-speaking ministers, accepting their religious expressions, offering them opportunities to exercise leadership in ministry after just one or two years of training. One commentator indicated that at least 15% of Hispanics have left the church in the past ten years.

Cultural Identity

I believe that the strongest reason why the immigrant people, and especially the Hispanics, leave the Catholic Church for the sects in this country is due to the problem of cultural identity.

We recognize that the church has made, and continues to make, many efforts to adapt to the new ethnic minorities, but so far they have been insufficient. And not everything that has been done is good. In many cases a pastoral of cultural assimilation has been offered—but sometimes it contains a type of paternalism that humiliates.

In the pastoral letter entitled *The Hispanic Presence: Challenge and Commitment* (1983), the U.S. bishops say:

> The universal character of the church involves both pluralism and unity. Humanity, in its cultures and peoples, is so various it could only have been crafted by the hand of God (#14)

and

> The Gospel teaching that no one is a stranger in the church is timeless. As the apostle Paul says, "There does not exist among you Jew or Greek, slave or freeman, male or female. All are one in Jesus Christ" (Gal 3:28). (#14)

The theory is clear enough, but not always practiced. Assimilation is a decisive element in the decision of minorities to join sects.

In addition to this, for cultural and at times racist reasons, people from minority groups are not welcomed into the church, or are treated as second-class Catholics. On the other hand, these same people are not only welcomed into the sects, but are actively sought out and invited.

The pastoral practice in many dioceses of lumping all minorities into a group labeled "multicultural" is done with good intentions, but it has hurt pastoral work tremendously. Everything is planned and carried out in the churches with the dominant culture in mind. The "multicultural" parishioners—the Japanese, the Latinos, the Koreans—have no power in the decision-making process. These people already have problems with discrimination and lack of power in the everyday world, and the problem is accentuated when they are treated in the same way in their church. This treatment serves as a painful reminder that they don't belong.

The enthusiasm for the multicultural concept comes from those who do not understand what it is like to be inside the melting pot. Multiculturalism does not go over well with those who have to live and suffer the consequences—those from the various countries and cultures.

The sects have not found it necessary to accept the multicultural concept. They try to adapt as much as possible to each minority group, making use of ministers who speak their language. Very soon these marginalized people are not only made to feel welcome, they are allowed to participate in ministries and to make decisions in their new church.

The Challenge of the Sects

Many people speak of how we Hispanics must defend against the threat of the cults and Pentecostalism, and if necessary prepare our people to respond and attack. But the focus has been poor—and wrong.

The sects, as I see it, are not a threat, nor an invasion, nor a fanaticism that will eventually go away. But they *are* a challenge to our pastoral focus and planning. The sects are showing us where the emptiness is in our pastoral thrust and evangelization efforts. In this sense they can be a help in alerting the Catholic Church to the need for making a move towards fashioning a church that is more personal, caring and communitarian—a church where everyone, regardless of race, ethnic background, or language, can feel needed and wanted and "at home."

FIFTEEN

Preaching in Spanish as a Second Language

Kenneth G. Davis

In the united states today, especially among roman Catholics, more and more non-native Spanish speakers are called upon to preach at least occasionally in Spanish. This article is an attempt to aid those involved in such an endeavor. Constraints of space dictate the somewhat artificial "how to" approach and, of course, nothing can substitute for fluency in the language and reflective experience with the Hispanic peoples.

Know the Assembly

Hispanics are a very complicated, mobile grouping of peoples. Not only do they embrace every race (*e.g.,* many of Caribbean descent are of African ancestry; many of Mexican descent have Native American forebears), but they now belong to, or are influenced by, a wide variety of Christian and non-Christian religions. Moreover, they are of disparate socio-economic backgrounds (generally, Cubans are more affluent; Puerto Ricans tend to be poorer), and come from different countries of origin. Add to this the great differences between their accommodation to the United States (*e.g.,* the monolingual Spanish-speaking immigrant versus the monolingual English-speaking, third-generation citizen), and one begins to appreciate how inadequate the umbrella term *Hispanic* is. Therefore, it is indispensable to know one's own specific assembly, preferably both through some quantitative survey as well as through lived, reflective experience.

I once preached at Mass and used United Farm Worker founder César Chávez as an example of a heroic Catholic who had successfully linked his faith with his everyday life. After Mass many a young man, usually a rather uninvolved bunch standing in the back, approached me and marveled at the fact that Señor Chávez was so influenced by the Faith. I was delighted by their interested comments. It was days later when someone explained to me that these young Mexicans thought I had been talking about a Mexican boxer by the same name! Chávez the farmworker is a Mexican-American (or Chicano), unfortunately wholly unknown to these recent Mexican immigrants. Although the Mexican and Chicano peoples' may both speak Spanish, be Catholic, live together, and share a common history, they are very different groups, and I erred by using an example inappropriate to that particular assembly. Hispanics are not interchangeable nor universal, and one must strive to know one's assembly well in order to use the symbols, slang, sayings, and historical anecdotes appropriate to a particular community.

Prepare Exegetically, Preach Poetically

There is no substitute for careful, prayerful preparation of the lectionary texts, and there are good Spanish-language exegetical tools listed, along with other resources, in Appendix One of this collection. However, the actual composition and delivery of the homily must respond to the *high context* reality of the Hispanic assembly. Appeals to the heart rather than dispassionate discourses are favored, as effective liturgy is more characterized by *ardor over order*. Word play, rhythm and rhyme, alliteration, metaphors—all the rhetorical tools aimed at motivating rather than informing need to be in the preacher's kit. This assembly is still generally more an oral rather than literate culture, and the popular wisdom expressed in devotions as well as kinetic symbols (palms, ashes, holy water, candles, incense, oil) must be blended into a deliberate but respectful attempt to evoke (without manipulating) an emotional response.

This is not to insult either the intelligence of the preacher or the assembly. *Preparation* of the homily requires research. But the composition and delivery must seek to touch the heart of the people. For a non-native this will require practice, revision, review by native speakers, and a humble willingness to learn through evaluation. I once borrowed an image from C.S. Lewis' *Chronicles of Narnia* and artfully wove the image of God as an untamed lion throughout the homily. I did not learn until it was too late that Spanish has two words for wild (*salvaje* refers to animals while *silvestre* describes plants), and I had woven the wrong adjective like a coarse, off-color thread throughout the consequently confused tapestry of my thought. Co-workers who can review the text, even listen to a live or recorded version of the homily, will be invaluable, which leads to the next and most important suggestion of all.

Form a Lectionary-Based Scripture Sharing Group

Those of us involved in the demanding ministry of preaching in a second language must apply ourselves diligently but also accept our limitations. We are not culturally a part of the community to whom we are called to serve as preacher. However, we must do everything possible to preach from within this reality which is why participating in a lectionary-based Scripture study group is indispensable. There are many models for forming and coordinating such groups; a good one is provided in the U.S. bishops' pastoral letter, *Fulfilled in Your Hearing: The Homily in the Sunday Assembly* (1982). Other resources include the various Spanish missalettes or the periodical *La Palabra Entre Nosotros* (see Appendix One, "Selected Pastoral Resources"). The idea is to listen to the people's reflection on the following week's readings, borrow from them, test ideas on them, consult with them, pray and dialogue with them and with the Scripture. Having had the experience of working with such a group, I would never again attempt to preach without them. It was such a group who insisted I preach on racism in the church because they had experienced it. Yet it was they who tempered my politically charged rhetoric because, in the history of their people, the church's involvement in politics had not always been a liberating experience. I had goodwill; they taught me good skills. It would be an imprudent, impudent, indeed impossible task to paint a word-picture without reflecting with the richly nuanced, many-hued reality of any Hispanic assembly. Not only has this been an ongoing source of deep personal insight, but I almost always come away with a summary statement for a homily, as well as with several good illustrations which I know will speak to the people because they came from the people. Once the Word is sown in such rich soil, all I have to do is water it with the perspiration of good exegetical preparation, allow someone to review the text or recording, and practice until I can deliver it confidently without notes. Such collaboration can, of course, have other important benefits, such as the creation of small Christian communities, and the empowering of these ministerial collaborators.

SIXTEEN

Religious Imagination

Alex García-Rivera

THERE WAS A TIME WHEN BEING HISPANIC AND BEING CATHOLIC were synonymous. Such a familiar correlation can no longer be made. Thousands of Hispanics are now members of other religious institutions—Protestant, Jehovah's Witness, Fundamentalist, Pentecostal—even Mormon. Such numbers, unfortunately, are more than converts to these groups but defections of former Roman Catholic Hispanics to institutions in which they have found a home.

Such large numbers of defections have alarmed the Catholic Church, and much blame is placed on the aggressive tactics of these institutions. Although I do agree that aggressive proselytism is part of the cause, it most certainly cannot carry the full share of explanation for this sad but true exodus of Hispanics from the Roman Catholic Church to other churches.

Total reliance on this reasoning would have one believe that Hispanics are fickle or swayed by sentiment or emotion rather than faith. No one who has seen the ardor, intelligence, and good works of these new Hispanic converts to other churches could maintain such a simplistic answer to this alarming phenomenon. It is, after all, not a Protestant problem or a Mormon problem but a Catholic problem. And we ought to at least entertain the most certain thought that perhaps the cause of this growing Hispanic exodus has its roots right here in the Catholic side of the promised land. I write this as a former member of that exodus, a former Lutheran pastor, who realized at last that the Catholic Church held the roots of my Hispanic Christian faith and returned.

94

The reason I left the church is the same reason I came back: the Catholic religious imagination. Let me explain. I am a Cuban refugee who was baptized, confirmed, and received first communion in the Roman Catholic Church in Cuba. Though pre-Vatican II, the Roman Catholic Church in Cuba was not some clone of a standard Latin ritual. We had our own brand of Catholicity. The *Virgen del Cobre* listened to our petitions, and San Martín de Porres comforted us in our trials.

This all changed when my family and I found ourselves exiled in the United States. The winds of change from Vatican II were just beginning to stir the entire church. Rightly so, Vatican II had called for the Mass to be said in the language of the people. Unfortunately for us, this meant English.

My alienation with the church increased when my family left Miami, where there were a lot of Cubans, and moved to Ohio, where there were almost none. Instead of finding nourishment and strength, I found misunderstanding and alienation. I left the church during my high-school years with the harsh judgment only teenagers are capable of having that the church itself was a spiritually bankrupt institution.

Several years later, I married a Lutheran woman who gently brought me back into the Christian Church, but it was not Catholic. I found the Lutheran Church very welcoming and inviting. I was treated with respect and encouraged to be Hispanic. This was easier said than done. As I got deeper into the life of the Lutheran Church, I found another type of alienation. It was not an alienation from the church but an alienation from myself, from my own roots as a Hispanic. No matter how hard I tried, the worship, the spirituality, even the famous hymn singing of the Lutherans could not reach the depths of my soul.

The Lutherans had a very tidy and biblical approach to their spirituality and tradition. This approach fit their Nordic backgrounds quite well. The Lutheran religious imagination worked wonders for those of northern European descent, but the imagination that fed my soul could not find a home there. Mine was fed by the Virgin of Guadalupe, Martín de Porres, meatless Fridays, and the *Vía Crucis*. I did find the Bible exciting, but it only came alive for me through my religious imagination. It eventually dawned on me that my harsh judgment of the Catholic Church had been done as a confused teenager in an alien environment. The English-speaking Catholic Church was but one brand of the Catholic religious imagination. What I had been searching for all along was my Hispanic Catholicity.

I returned to the Roman Catholic Church to rediscover it. I returned to a very different church from the one I had left. If the Catholic Church is losing Hispanics to other churches, it may be, in part, because they are discovering now-rapidly disappearing parts of the Catholic Church that once fed and sustained Hispanic religiosity. Now these elements are being discouraged or, even, looked down upon by an increasingly modern church. The fundamental problem is that the modern Catholic Church is increasingly losing touch with the religious imagination. The emphasis on "proper" liturgical procedure, for example, has discouraged the continuation of messy, sentimental, "improper" liturgies common to Hispanic popular religion. A case in point is the mini-conflict my Hispanic community experienced recently during Advent.

As it happened, the Third Sunday of Advent coincided with the very popular Hispanic feast of Our Lady of Guadalupe. The liturgical director of our church kept insisting that none of the regular Sunday services could be changed because "proper" liturgical practice gave priority to the Sunday celebration. The "local" celebration of Our Lady of Guadalupe would be improper. Finally we were able to persuade her to allow an extraordinary Mass to be celebrated at 5 a.m. in honor of Our Lady of Guadalupe, which would not interfere with the already planned Advent Masses. I suppose part of what persuaded her was the belief that no one would come to a 5 a m. Mass in the middle of winter. It became obvious that Sunday that this particular liturgical director did not understand the religious imagination.

At a quarter to 5, the vans and cars of the Hispanic community began to arrive to begin the Mass by singing the *Mananitas* ("the little morning") to Our Lady. A crowd had gathered at the front of the church when the priest walked out to greet us. His jaw dropped when he saw the entire block covered with people, men, women, and children, even infants, standing in the chill of that December 12 before the sun had yet risen. As we processed in, the church became filled. There was standing room only. The religious imagination had captured the Hispanic dimension of the Catholic Church and delivered it at the altar.

The modern Catholic Church is in danger of losing this imagination. The Hispanic exodus is one of the symptoms. Lest I be misunderstood, let me state that I am not against the practice of the liturgical year. The liturgical year, on the other hand, used to be full of the religious imagination. The liturgical year used to be significantly modulated by the martyrology of the church. Saints' feasts sometimes took precedence over the Sunday liturgy. Now it seems, the modern Catholic Church is embarrassed by her saints and her angels. Even the Virgin of Guadalupe of Hispanic religion tends to embarrass some of our religious leaders. Moreover, the liturgical year included what the church would now classify as non-liturgical celebrations: the local feasts and traditions that gave not only color and vitality to the church but also were a mark of its catholicity. Many of these feasts and local traditions did not fall on a Sunday.

The religious imagination is part of the antidote to the Hispanic exodus. If Hispanics are finding a home in other churches, then, ironically, the reason may be that they have been more successful at capturing the Hispanic Catholic imagination than the Catholic Church has. It is this imagination that has allowed the church to survive these 2,000 years through a myriad of crises and to thrive in a multitude of cultures. The Hispanic exodus ought to alarm the church not because other churches are stealing their flock but, rather, that the Catholic religious imagination may be dimming.

SEVENTEEN

Spirituality

Arturo Pérez Rodríguez

C.P.M. JONES WISELY STATES THAT "IN SPIRITUALITY, THERE ARE ultimately no 'rules of the game,' even those laid down by the saints, but only 'tips of the trade,' freely offered to be freely available, to those who need them, sometimes permanently and sometimes in a passing stage of development" ("Liturgy and Personal Devotion," *The Study of Spirituality,* eds. Jones, Wainright, and Arnold, New York: Oxford, 1986, 6). The following essay offers tips, hints, and possible ways for understanding Hispanic spirituality "to those who need them." The first tip concerns the term "Hispanic"; second is an attempt to define spirituality from the Hispanic perspective; third, characteristics of Hispanic spirituality; and finally spiritual issues facing the Hispanic community.

Hispanic or Latino or . . .

Both the terms "Hispanic" and "Latino" are problematic in that they refer to a diverse people. Allan Figueroa Deck demonstrates why both must be used with caution. "For the purpose of dividing Hispanic communities into more workable groupings, one might conceive of them in terms of five historical and geographical divisions:

(1) those whose origins are to be found in Middle America, especially Mexico;

(2) Central Americans;

(3) the Caribbean people (Cubans, Puerto Ricans, and Do-minicans);

(4) the Andean peoples, and

(5) the Borderlands peoples of the American Southwest and California ("Hispanic Catholics: Historical Explora-tions and Cultural Analysis," *U.S. Catholic Historian* 9 [Winter/Spring 1990]: 138).

The Hispanic people are diverse not only in their geo-graphic and cultural background but also in their identification within the Hispanic community itself. Some Southwestern His-panic families trace their histories to this land before the United States existed. Other Hispanics have disassociated themselves from the Spanish language, Hispanic culture and community for a vast array of reasons. They are foreigners among their own. There are others who see themselves as a new race of people—a U.S. Hispanic *mestizo,* a blend of the peoples of the past formed by the realities of the present. The diversity of the Hispanic com-munity is its strength insofar as it reflects and incorporates many different peoples into one.

There are points of convergence that help to untie the His-panic community. The most basic point is one of common ori-gin: from the painful birthing act of the 16th-century Spanish conquest, a new life issued forth. The religious spirit of the in-digenous pre-Columbian/African people grafted with the Chris-tian faith of the Spanish evangelizers roots Hispanic spirituality.

Another point of convergence is what we might call the *mestizo* (Virgilio Elizondo, *The Future is Mestizo,* New York: Crossroad, 1992) way of mixing various experiences to form a "third way." Life is not seen as black or white, either-or, one or the other, but as "perhaps," "maybe," "possibly this way." This per-spective, this pattern of living, shapes the Hispanic spiritual reality.

There is one other point that is important to make when defining the Hispanic community. Formerly this community was universally thought to be Roman Catholic. With the successful evangelization by various fundamentalist and evangelical denomi-nations, Roman Catholicism can no longer be presumed. Yet even here the dynamic of *mestizaje* (mixing) that is characteristic of the Hispanic community cannot be underestimated. Though we will continue to use the term "Hispanic" in this article, in reality we are speaking about a new *mestizo* spirituality that is blended from all these experiences. Let us consider our second tip, how the Hispanic community defines spirituality.

Attempting a Definition

Definitions of spirituality can seduce us into believing that we can fully comprehend a religious experience. By attempting to define Hispanic spirituality, we may be tempted to think that we can control—even dominate—our relationship with God. The challenge at hand is to articulate in understandable categories something of the spiritual pattern that is etched in the Hispanic person while acknowledging that the ways of the Spirit are beyond definition and our control. Three persons attempt a definition.

Ricardo Ramírez places spirituality *within* the mystery of the human person. He writes,

Spirituality for any group of people refers to the "inner space" or internal spiritual processes that allow people to come in touch with themselves as "believing." It refers to the area of life where the divine spirit touches the human spirit, where the redemption happens as the person recognizes the transcendent in his or her own life. . . . For Hispanics, this faith experience that is at the heart of spirituality touches not only the spiritual . . . but it is also one that affects their total lives. . . . It brings (Hispanic) people in touch with the past spirituality of their ancestors. ("Hispanic Spirituality," *Social Thought* 9 [Summer 1985]: 6).

This "inner space" emphasis becomes a dynamic of seeking, searching, and stretching oneself in ways that define the Hispanic person's relationship with God and with the community. The word to emphasize in this definition is *touch*—something characteristic of Hispanic spirituality.

Deck speaks of spirituality ". . . as encompassing all those ways in which the Christian faithful pursue and deepen their life of faith in Christ within the Christian community" ("Hispanic

Catholics," 140). *All those ways* carries a sense of inclusivity. Whatever puts a person *in contact* with the Christ of their life is included in a definition of spirituality. This means suspending judgments about traditional, cultural, popular religious expressions that from an outsider's (non-Hispanic) point of view might be considered superstitious, uninformed, or overly pietistic. It also means assessing and valuing familial patterns of prayer, even if they are practiced in English. Deck clearly states that this inclusivity requires "a sense of awe and contemplation in the face of the mystery of God" ("Hispanic Catholics," 141). Both Ramírez and Deck regard popular religious expressions as keys for entering into a relationship with the God of our lives.

Rosa María Icaza's definition, based on the *National Pastoral Plan for Hispanic Ministry* (1987), identifies spirituality as "the orientation and perspective of all dimensions of a person's life in the following of Jesus, moved by the Spirit, and in continuous dialogue with the Father" ("Spirituality of the Mexican American People," *Worship* 63 [May 1989]: 232). Once again the theme of inclusivity lights the way as Icaza affirms *the orientation and perspective of all dimensions of a person's life.* There is a dialogue of life, an interaction of people, an emotional interchange that motivates the relationship between the Hispanic person, God, and the community at large. Icaza says "It seems, then, that for Hispanics, spirituality is translated into the love of God which moves, strengthens and is manifested in love of neighbor and self." Love binds a people together no matter how diverse they may be. This common experience of the Hispanic community, being loved by God, fashions us into *El Pueblo de Dios,* the People of God.

General Characteristics

Touch, inclusiveness, love of God, self and neighbor translate into specific characteristics of Hispanic spirituality. Using the *Pastoral Plan,* Icaza delineates these characteristics:

> (1) A basic and constant aspect is a sense of the presence of God.

(2) God is found in the arms of the Virgin Mary. She is at the heart of spirituality.

(3) The "seeds of the Word" in pre-Hispanic cultures are still cultivated.

(4) Spirituality is expressed in popular devotions and in the use of symbols and gestures.

(5) It is also expressed in behavior revealing Gospel values, such as prayer and hospitality, endurance and hope, commitment and forgiveness.

(6) Faith is kept alive at home through practices in daily life and particularly during the principal seasons of the liturgical year.

(7) All celebrations are seen as communal and most of them include prayer, sharing food, and singing/dancing/reciting or composing poetry.

(8) Finally, Hispanics seldom pray for themselves but regularly for others. They often request others to remember them in their prayers.

I would add the following clarifications:

(9) Hispanic spirituality is "touchable," incarnational. Body, soul, and Spirit are seen as one. Oftentimes this is referred to as "fiesta," where all that is contained in life (including death) is embraced and celebrated. This unity of body, soul, and Spirit is what makes sense of healings—physical, emotional, and spiritual—and those who administer them, the faithhealers of the Hispanic community, *curanderos, santeros,* etc.

(10) Spiritual intimacy relates and reveals us to one another, thus forming familial and extrafamilial relationships between ourselves and with God.

(11) There is a personal and communal sense of sin, culpability, and evil.

(12) Hispanic spirituality is related to four sacramental moments: baptism, eucharist (specifically in first communion), marriage and anointing (inclusive of the funeral rites of the church and Hispanic community).

(13) Oral traditions, namely *dichos* (sayings), popular songs and traditional sacred religious hymns, shared family religious histories, dramas, and festivals form Hispanic wisdom literature.

(14) Contemplation and mysticism are characteristic marks of Hispanic spirituality. "The sense of mystery and awe, of contemplative and mystical interiority are part of the Hispanic soul" (German Martínez, "Hispanic Culture and Worship: The Process of Inculturation," *U.S. Catholic Historian* 11 [Spring 1993]: 88).

These characteristics come to life and become the language of prayer when they are expressed "rite-fully" in the diversity of Hispanic popular religion. "The fundamental expression of that spirituality is popular devotion (popular religion), not the refined asceticism, profound mysticism, or elaborate spiritualities of great writers, mystics, and saints" (Deck, "Hispanic Catholics," 141).

Issues Facing Hispanic Spirituality

Mestizaje is only achieved at great price. As was true in the 16th century, the birthing of a U.S. Hispanic *mestizo* spirituality requires great sacrifice. Though there are many concerns, three specific issues suggest approaches for the future.

(1) "A core spiritual issue facing each and every Hispanic, whether he or she be of Mexican, Cuban, Puerto Rican, or other Latin American extraction, is how to relate to the dominant culture and to one's culture of origin." (Juan-Lorenzo Hinojosa, "Culture, Spirituality, and United States Hispanics," *Frontiers of Hispanic Theology in the United States,* Maryknoll: Orbis, 1992, 155). Hispanics, be they Spanish-speaking only, bilingual, or English-speaking only face the constant influence of the dominant culture as well as the influence of other racial and ethnic

groups. Each group has its own spirituality, popular expressions of prayer and experiences of God. *Mestizaje* means mixing: not assimilating or disappearing but blending with these other spiritual realities. *Mestizo* spirituality is expressed best in *mestizo* liturgy, a form of prayer that allows the Hispanic faith experience to be heard, seen, touched, smelled, savored, and embraced by those at prayer.

(2) Popular religion is a living language of prayer that will continue to evolve into new ways, forms, and expressions. Popular religious practices based on "what has always been" may not necessarily be appropriate for the future. One example of this is the experience of Hispanic popular religious practices celebrated in English. The change in language, from Spanish to English, affects the silent "inner spaces" of life. The "touch" that is felt between the community, God, and one another is lived out in a new way. The language of prayer, as it develops and changes, will continue to be an issue in the spiritual life of the Hispanic community.

(3) The third issue is the simple acknowledgment that Hispanic spirituality does indeed exist. Can we, Hispanic or non-Hispanic alike, accept and affirm it as an authentic school of spirituality, as much as the Ignatian, Franciscan, Teresian or any other school of spirituality? This school of spirituality is more easily found in pilgrimages of faith, in Good Friday living stations of the cross, in the Hispanic rites of marriage, in all that makes life holy and acknowledges the presence of God.

Hispanic spirituality touches the center of life, the heart of the Hispanic community. It offers "spiritual tips" to the larger U.S. Catholic community and the opportunity to testify to the diversity of God's life. "Since the spiritual crisis of modernity is rooted in the loss of the symbolic, the transcendent and the communal characteristics of Hispanic spirituality, Hispanic wisdom can make an important contribution to the renewal of the spiritual wealth of the American Churches searching today for a new post-modern experience of faith" (Martínez, "Hispanic Culture and Worship," 91).

EIGHTEEN

Popular Religion

Virgilio Elizondo

THE MEXICAN AMERICAN IN THE UNITED STATES IS ONE WHO
through birth or acquired nationality is *a citizen of the United
States while maintaining a deep Mexican heritage.* Today there
are approximately 14,300,000 Mexican Americans in the United
States, and the number continues to increase daily. It is a highly
complex socio-cultural group that is quite at home in the United
States without ever fully assimilating the U.S. way of life. It is
neither fully North American nor fully Latin American. It lived in
its present day geographical setting long before the United States
migrated west and took over the Mexican territories. One of the
key factors in the group identity, cohesiveness and continuity of
the group is the persistence of its religious symbolism, which we
will explore briefly in this presentation.

Function of Religious Symbols

The popular expressions of the faith *function in totally
different ways for various peoples, depending on their history
and socio-cultural status.* For the dominant culture, the popular
expressions of the faith will serve to legitimize their way of life as
God's true way for humanity. They will tranquilize the moral conscience and blind people from seeing the injustices which exist in
daily life. For a colonized/oppressed/dominated group, they are
the ultimate resistance to the attempts of the dominant culture to
destroy them as a distinct group either through annihilation or
through absorption and total assimilation. They will maintain

alive the sense of injustice to which the people are subjected in their daily lives.

By popular expressions of the faith, I do not refer to the private or individual devotions of a few people but to the *ensemble of beliefs, rituals, ceremonies, devotions and prayers which are commonly practiced by the people at large*. It is my contention, which is beyond the scope of this paper to develop but which will be its point of departure, that those expressions of the faith which are celebrated voluntarily by the majority of the people, transmitted from generation to generation by the people themselves and which go on with the church, without it or even in spite of it, express the *deepest identity of the people*. They are the ultimate foundation of the people's innermost being and the common expression of the collective soul of the people. They are supremely meaningful for the people who celebrate them and meaningless to the outsider. To the people whose very life-source they are, no explanation is necessary, but to the casual or scientific spectator no explanation will ever express or communicate their true and full meaning. Without them, there might be associations of individuals bound together by common interest (*e.g.,* the corporation, the State, etc.), but there will never be the experience of being a people.

It is within the context of the tradition of the group that one experiences both a sense of selfhood and a sense of *belonging*. Furthermore it is within the tradition that one remains in contact both with one's beginnings through the genealogies and the stories of origins and with one's ultimate end. We are born into them and within them we discover our full and ultimate being. I might enjoy and admire other traditions very much, but I will never be fully at home within them. No matter how much I get into them, I will always have a sense of being other.

From the very beginning, Christianity presented a very unique way of universalizing peoples without destroying their localized identity. People would neither have to disappear through assimilation nor be segregated as inferior. The Christian message interwove with the local religious traditions so as to give the people a deeper sense of local identity (a sense of rootedness), while at the same time breaking down the psycho-sociological barriers that kept nationalities separate and apart from each other so as to allow for a truly universal fellowship (a sense of universality). In other words, it *affirmed rootedness while destroying ghettoishness.* Christianity changed peoples and cultures not by destroying them, but by reinterpreting their core rituals and myths through the foundational ritual and myth of Christianity. Thus, now a Jew could still be a faithful Jew and yet belong fully to the new universal fellowship, and equally a Greek or a Roman could still be fully Greek or Roman and equally belong to the new universal group.

Religious Traditions of the Americas

The beginning of the Americas introduces two *radically distinct image/myth representations* of the Christian tradition. The United States *was born as a secular enterprise* with a deep sense of religious mission. Native religions were eliminated and totally supplanted by a new type of religion: Puritan moralism, Presbyterian righteousness and Methodist social consciousness coupled with deism and the spirit of rugged individualism to provide a sound basis for the new nationalism which would function as the core religion of the land. It was *quite different in Latin America* where the religion of the old world clashed with those of the new and, in their efforts to uproot the native religions, Iberian Catholics found themselves totally assumed into them. Iberian Catholicism, with its emphasis on clerical rituals and the divinely established monarchical nature of all society, conquered physically but itself *was absorbed by the pre-Colombian spiritualism* with its emphasis on the harmonious unity of opposing tensions: male and female, suffering and happiness, self-annihilation and transcendence, individual and group, sacred and profane. In the secular-based culture of the United States, it is the one who succeeds materially who appears to be the upright and righteous person—the good and saintly. In the pre-Colombian/Iberian-Catholic *mestizo*-based culture of Mexico, it is the one who can endure all the opposing tensions of life and not lose his or her interior harmony who appears to be the upright and righteous one.

With the great western expansion of the United States in the 1800s, *half of northern Mexico was conquered* and taken over by the United States. The Mexicans living in the vast region spanning a territory of over 3,500 kilometers from California to Texas suddenly became aliens in their own land . . . foreigners who never left home. Their entire way of life was despised. The Mexican *mestizo* was abhorred as a mongrel who was good only for cheap labour. Efforts were instituted to *suppress everything Mexican: customs, language and Mexican Catholicism.* The fair-skinned, blond Mexicans who remained had the choice of assimilating totally to the white, Anglo-Saxon Protestant culture of the United States or being ostracized as an inferior human being. The dark-skinned had no choice! They were marked as an inferior race destined to be the servants of the white master race.

Today, social unrest and dire poverty force many people from Mexico to move to the former Mexican territories which politically are part of the United States. Newcomers are harrassed by the immigration services of the United States as illegal intruders—a curious irony since it was the United States who originally entered this region illegally and stole it from Mexico. Yet the descendants of the original settlers of this region, plus those who have immigrated, continue to feel at home, to resist efforts of destruction through assimilation and to celebrate their legitimacy as a people.

Mexican American Religious Symbols

The Mexican Americans living in that vast borderland between the United States and Mexico have *not only survived* as a unique people but *have even maintained good mental health* in spite of the countless insults and put-downs suffered throughout its history and even in the present moment of time. Anyone who has suffered such a long history of segregation, degradation and exploitation should be a mental wreck. Yet, despite their ongoing suffering, not only are the numbers increasing, but in general they are prospering, joyful and healthy, thanks to the profound faith of the people as lived and expressed through the common religious practices of the group. I could explore many of them, but I will limit myself to what I consider to be the *three sets of related core expressions* which mark the ultimate ground, the perimeters and the final aspirations of the Mexican-American people: *Guadalupe/Baptism; dust/water; crucifixion/the "dead" ones.* They are the symbols in which the apparently destructive forces of life are assumed, transcended and united. In them, we experience the ultimate meaning and destiny of our life pilgrimage.

There is no greater and more persistent symbol of Mexican and Mexican-American identity than devotion to Our Lady of Guadalupe. Thousands visit her home at Tepeyac each day and she keeps reappearing daily throughout the Americas in the spontaneous prayers and artistic expressions of the people. In her, the people experience acceptance, dignity, love and protection . . . they dare to affirm life even when all others deny them life. Since her apparition, she has been the flag of all the great movements of Independence, betterment and liberty.

Were it not for Our Lady of Guadalupe there would be no Mexican or Mexican-American people today. The great Mexican nations had been defeated by the Spanish invasion which came to a violent and bloody climax in 1521. The native peoples who had not been killed no longer wanted to live. Everything of value to them, including their gods, had been destroyed. Nothing was worth living for. With this colossal catastrophe, their entire past became irrelevant. New diseases appeared and, together with the trauma of the collective death-wish of the people, the native population decreased enormously.

It was in *the brown Virgin of Guadalupe that Mexicanity was born* and through her that the people have survived and developed. At the very moment when the pre-Colombian world had come to a drastic end, a totally unsuspected irruption took place in 1531 when, in the ancient site of the goddess Tonantzin, a *mestizo* woman appeared to announce a new era for "all the inhabitants of this land." Guadalupe provides the spark which will allow the people to arise out of the realm of death, like the rising phoenix arising out of the ashes of the past—not just a return to the past but the emergence of a spectacular newness. In sharp contrast to the total rupture with the past which was initiated by the conquest-evangelization enterprise, Guadalupe provided the necessary *sense of continuity* which is basic to human existence. Since the apparition took place at Tepeyac, the long-venerated site of the goddess Tonantzin, it put people in direct contact with their ancient past and in communion with their own foundational mythology. It validated their ancestry while initiating them into something new. The missioners had said their ancestors had been wrong and that the diabolical past had to be totally eradicated. But the lady who introduced herself as the mother of the true God was now appearing among them and asking that a *temple* be built on this sacred site. Out of their own past and in close continuity with it, something truly sacred was now emerging.

Furthermore, she was giving meaning to the present moment in several ways for she was promising them love, defense and protection. At a time when the people had experienced the abandonment of their gods, the mother of the true God was now offering them her personal intervention. At a time when new racial and ethnic divisions were emerging, she was offering the basis of a new unity as the mother of all the inhabitants of the land. At a time when the natives were being instructed and told what to do by the Spaniards, she chose a low-class Indian to be her trusted messenger who was to instruct the Spaniards through the person of the bishop and tell them what to do.

Finally, she initiated and proclaimed the new era which was now beginning. Over her womb is the Aztec glyph for the center of the universe. Thus she carries the force which will gradually build up the civilization which will be neither a simple restoration of the past nor simply New Spain but the beginning of something new. The sign of flowers, which she provided as a sign of her authenticity, was for the Indian world the sign which guaranteed that the new life would truly flourish.

Thus in Guadalupe, the *ancient beginnings connect with the present moment and point to what is yet to come!* The broken pieces of their ancient numinous world are now re-pieced in a totally new way. Out of the chaos, a new world of ultimate meaning is now emerging. The phoenix had truly come forth not just as a powerful new life, but also as the *numinosum* which would allow them to once again experience the awe and reverence of the sacred—not a sacred which was foreign and opposed to them, but one which ultimately legitimized them in their innermost being—both collectively as a people and individually as persons.

The second great religious expression is the baptism of infants. Our Lady of Guadalupe had sent the Indian Juan Diego to the church. The Indian world immediately started to go to church and ask for baptism. Yet, they were no longer being up-rooted totally from their ancient ways in order to enter the church. They were entering as they were—with their customs, their rituals, their songs, their dances and their pilgrimages. The old Franciscan missioners feared this greatly. Many thought it was a devil's trick to subvert their missionary efforts. But the people kept on coming. They were truly building the new temple the Lady had requested: the living temple of Mexican Christians. It is through baptism that every newborn Mexican enters personally into the temple requested by the Lady. Through baptism the child becomes part of the continuum and is guaranteed life in spite of the social forces against life. The community claims the child as its very own and with pride presents it to the entire people. In the group, the child will receive great affirmation and tenderness. This will give the child a profound sense of existential security. He/she will be able to affirm selfhood despite the put-downs and insults of society: they will dare to be who they are—and they will be who they are with a great sense of pride!

The ashes of the beginning of Lent are a curious and mysterious religious expression of the Mexican tradition which finds its full socio-religious meaning when coupled with the holy water blessed during the Easter Vigil. For people who have been forced to become foreigners in their own land, who have been driven from their properties and who have been pushed around by the powerful in the way the mighty wind blows the dust around, ashes, as a moment of the continuum of the pilgrimage of life, become most powerful. They mark the radical acceptance of the moment—actually there is no choice. But this is not the end, for the people do not only come for ashes. Throughout the year they come for *holy water* to sprinkle upon themselves, their children, their homes . . . everything. They are very aware that our entire world yearns and travails in pain awaiting to be redeemed—a redemption which in Christ has indeed begun but whose rehabilitating effects are yet to take effect in our world of present-day injustices. The sprinkling with the waters of the Easter Vigil is a constant call for the *regeneration of all of creation*.

The dust which is sprinkled with the water will be turned into fertile earth and produce in great abundance. As in the reception of ashes there is an acceptance, in the sprinkling of holy water there is an unquestioned affirmation: the ashes will again become earth; the dust-people will become the fertile earth and the earth will once again be ours. The *dust-water binomial* symbolizes the great suffering of an uprooted people who refuse to give in to despair but live in the unquestioned hope of the new life that is sure to come.

The final set of religious celebrations which express the core identity of the Mexican-American people is the crucifixion which is celebrated on Good Friday and the dead whose day is celebrated on November 2. For a people who have consistently been subjected to injustice, cruelty, and early death, the image of the crucified is the supreme symbol of life despite the multiple daily threats of death. If there was something good and redemptive in the unjust condemnation and crucifixion of the God-man, then, as senseless and useless as our suffering appears to be, there must be something of ultimate goodness and transcendent value in it. We don't understand it, but in Jesus, the God-man who suffered for our salvation, we affirm it and in this very affirmation receive the power to endure it without it destroying us. *Even if we are killed, we cannot be destroyed.* This is the curious irony of our celebrations of the dead: they appear to be dead, but they are not really dead! For they live not only in God but in our hearts and in our memory. Those whom the world thinks are dead . . . those who have been killed by society . . . defy death and are alive in us. In our celebrations of memory, their presence is keenly experienced. Thus what is celebrated as the day of the dead is in effect the celebration of life—a life which not even death can destroy. Society might take our lands away, marginate us and even kill us, but it cannot destroy us. For we live on in the generations to come and in them we continue to be alive.

Conclusion

The *conquest of ancient Mexico by Spain in 1521* and then the *conquest of northwest Mexico by the United States in the 1840s* forced the native population and their succeeding generations into a split and meaningless existence. It was a mortal collective catastrophe of gigantic death-bearing consequences. Yet the people have survived as a people through the *emergence of new religious symbols* and the reinterpretation of old ones which have connected the past with the present and projected into the future. The core religious expressions as celebrated and transmitted by the people are the unifying symbols in which the opposing forces of life are brought together into a harmonious tension so as to give the people who participate in them the experience of *wholeness.* In them and through them, opposites are brought together and push towards a resolution, and the people who celebrate them experience an overcoming of the split. Where formerly there was opposition, now there is reconciliation and even greater yet, synthesis. This is precisely what gives joy and meaning to life, indeed makes life possible in any meaningful sense regardless of the situation. It is in the celebration of these festivals of being and memory that the people live on as a people.

NINETEEN

Liturgy

Timothy M. Matovina

A 1985 SURVEY OF HISPANIC CATHOLICS THROUGHOUT THE UNITED States indicated that 55% of those surveyed had never heard of Vatican II. This statistic implies that most Hispanic Catholics in this country are unaware of the council's call for liturgical reform in the first of its decrees. Yet pastoral agents frequently note that Hispanic faith communities evidence a vibrant liturgical life. Though not always cognizant of magisterial directives, Hispanic Catholics apparently sense the call to worship that those directives promote. Their ritual life illuminates three elements of liturgy that enhance devotion and faith in U.S. Hispanic communities.

Liturgy: An Encounter with the Person of Jesus

At San Fernando Cathedral in San Antonio, Texas. a growing tradition among the primarily Mexican-American congregation is a Good Friday passion drama. The youth and other parishioners lead this liturgy, which begins in the public market, winds through the city's downtown streets and ends with the crucifixion on the steps of the cathedral.

During one such procession, from among the thousands gathered, a three-year-old child spontaneously stepped forward to wipe the face of Jesus. Like this child's act of compassion, Hispanic devotions such as the way of the cross (vía crucis), the seven last words of Jesus (las siete palabras) and the entombment (servicio del santo entierro) are acts of worship that unite the community with the suffering Jesus. Similarly, when Hispanics place the child Jesus in the crib *(acostada del niño),* offer their devotion at the manger scene *(nacimiento)* or recall the worship of the shepherds in a Christmas drama *(la pastorela),* they encounter a human Jesus who is tangible and approachable. These expressions of faith enable Hispanics to accompany Jesus during the most vulnerable moments of His life.

As the U.S. bishops stated in their 1983 pastoral, *The Hispanic Presence: Challenge and Commitment:* "Hispanic spirituality places strong emphasis on the humanity of Jesus, especially when He appears weak and suffering, as in the crib and in His passion and death" (#12). In light of the poverty and discrimination many Hispanics endure, this is not surprising.

Liturgy: Prophetic Fiesta

Several years ago I attended the 50th anniversary celebration of a Mexican-American couple. At the end of the eucharist, Doña Librada, the wife, thanked the guests for attending. She mentioned that all of her grandchildren and great-grandchildren were present, as were 11 of her 12 children. The missing child was her son Cruz, who had called from prison the night before. Doña Librada told us that her heart was full of joy to see so many relatives and friends together and that such gatherings were her greatest comfort as she grew older. But, she added, her joy could not be complete because her son Cruz was not with her, and because "the heart of a mother feels most for the child who is absent."

Doña Librada's words express a profound element of eucharistic and other liturgical fiestas. While we are called to gather in great joy as God's people, our heart must yearn for sisters and brothers who are absent or troubled. Hispanic rites like *las posadas* reflect this understanding of liturgy. The *posadas* are Advent novena celebrations that reenact the pilgrimage of Mary and Joseph on the way to Bethlehem. Participants accompany Mary and Joseph seeking *posada* ("shelter") at various homes. They are rejected at all but the last, where they enter and partake in a communal fiesta. This fiesta celebrates the joy of accepting pilgrims whom the world rejects. Like Doña Librada's words, the *posada* reminds us that our joy is not complete until we receive the rejected and forgotten into our lives.

Liturgy: Extending the Family of God

The inclusion of *padrinos* ("godparents") in sacramental rites is a consistent concern of Hispanic families, but *padrinos* are chosen not just for baptism and confirmation, but also for first communion, marriage and the maturing to adulthood of a young woman *(quinceañera)*. The significance of *padrinos* for Hispanics is evidenced in the number of *padrinos* chosen (for example, in marriages there are usually at least five or six couples) and the concern that they occupy a prominent place in the celebration. This liturgical inclusion expresses solidarity between family members and others incorporated into a family group. In this ritual incorporation parents and *padrinos* become *compadres* (literally, "co-parents"), forming a spiritual bond that extends familial relations. This bond is reinforced in a fiesta continuing the sacramental celebration, for which the *compadres* provide financial and other support.

This Hispanic sense of family extended in ritual is seen also in remembrances of Mary, the saints and the dead. Rosaries, home altars with their multiple images of the Virgin and saints, the *pésame* ("condolence") offered to the Virgin on Good Friday, the blessing of graves and novenas held after a loved one dies are visible reminders that those who have gone before us are still family members. The Hispanic preference for numerous statues and images in churches stems in large part from this understanding of liturgy as an extension of familial ties into the community of believers, both past and present. As the U.S. bishops said in their 1987 *National Pastoral Plan for Hispanic Ministry:* "The Hispanic people find God in the arms of the Virgin Mary. . . . The saints, our brothers and sisters who have already fulfilled their lives in the following of Jesus, are examples and instruments of the revelation of God's goodness through their intercession and help. All this makes Hispanic spirituality a home of living relationships, a family, a community" (#94).

Unfortunately, some liturgists and pastoral agents see these elements of Hispanic worship as detrimental to liturgical reform. Devotions to Jesus in the crib and on the cross have been characterized as sentimental, sensational, and as hindering authentic celebration of the Incarnation and the paschal mystery. The festive spirit of Hispanic assemblies is sometimes regarded as incongruent with the "noble simplicity" of liturgical rites emphasized by Vatican II, and attempts to renew sacramental celebrations and worship space can easily overlook Hispanic efforts to extend the family in ritual, art and environment.

Other liturgists and pastoral agents view Hispanic ritual in a more positive light. They recognize that continuing liturgical education is imperative for all the faithful (*Constitution on the Sacred Liturgy,* #19), but that the council also calls the church's ministers to "respect and foster the genius and talents of the various races and peoples" in liturgical celebrations (#37). This approach promotes the liturgical reform decreed by the council, but also enhances authentic elements of liturgical tradition already embodied in Hispanic ritual life.

TWENTY

Pastoral de Conjunto

Ana María Pineda

THE TERM *PASTORAL DE CONJUNTO* REPRESENTS THE HISTORICAL process of evangelization which has occurred among U.S. Hispanic Catholics since 1972. It marks the genius of U.S. Hispanic Catholicism, but how is this so? Where does the term *pastoral de conjunto* come from? What does it mean? How has it affected the understanding of church among Hispanics? What is its contribution to the church and society today?

History of a Concept

Pastoral de Conjunto as a concept is not new. It is rooted in the Gospel imperative of communion and unity. It permeates the Vatican II deliberations as it underscores communion and catholicity. It is explicitly stated in the documents of Medellín and Puebla.

It was Medellín's serious and realistic examination of the situation in Latin America in light of Vatican II that led the Latin American hierarchy to acknowledge the poverty of the masses caused by the existing social and political structures. This grave reality challenged the Latin American church to consider anew the mission of the church to bring all humankind to the fullness of communion of life with God. In order to be faithful to its mission, conversion of persons and structures would be urgent. The common salvific activity of the church needed to be directed in such a way as to bring about the transformation of society and of itself as the family of God. The document of Medellín explained that this could only be accomplished by using an integrated approach to pastoral work. Diverse ministries not only must be at the service of the unity of communion, but in doing so must constitute itself and act in solidarity (#7, 219). Ten years later, the conference held in Puebla addressed in part the experience of conflict occurring in pastoral activity due often to a lack of overall integration, lack of community support, the lack of sufficient preparation for work in the social sphere, or the lack of maturity in dealing with such experiences (#122). In order to avoid such conflict, it was necessary to encourage groups, communities, and movements to work consciously toward a pastoral style that stressed coordination and collaboration. This required that all the persons concerned participate at every level in a reflective process of faith which led to praxis. As a consequence of such reflection, the document of Puebla is able to describe the concept of *pastoral de conjunto* as:

> A well-planned pastoral effort is the specific, conscious, deliberate response to the necessities of evangelization. It should be implemented through a process of participation at every level of the communities and persons concerned. They must be taught how to analyze reality, how to reflect on this reality from the standpoint of the Gospel, how to choose the most suitable objectives and means, and how to use them in the most sensible way for the work of evangelization (#1307).

Chronologically, however, the conference held in Puebla in 1979 was preceded by the *II Encuentro Nacional Hispano de Pastoral* in the United States in 1977.

The Term "Pastoral de Conjunto"

The term *pastoral de conjunto* took on special significance for U.S. Hispanic Catholics during the process of pastoral assessment initiated by the three national convocations of Hispanic lay and religious leaders known as the *Encuentros Nacionales Hispanos de Pastoral* held in 1972, 1977, and 1985. The *Encuentros* sought to give voice to a disenfranchised sector of the U.S. Catholic Church. In doing so, they stressed the importance of each person and of the community at large in living and being church. The process of the *Encuentros* required broad participation by the people, small communities, and small groups; team work; integration of different pastoral areas; a common vision; interrelating among the dioceses, regions, and the national level; openness to the needs of the people and to the universality of the church (*National Pastoral Plan for Hispanic Ministry*, 1987, #19). As a consequence of such a challenging process, Hispanics experienced what it meant to live the church as communion. It is within this context that the term *pastoral de conjunto* began to appear in the documents of the *Encuentro Nacional Hispano de Pastoral*. The search to belong to the church—not only by virtue of their longstanding tradition of faith, but as fully incorporated family members with all of the accompanying rights and responsibilities—had led Hispanic Catholics to appropriate the term *pastoral de conjunto* that had been used in the Medellín documents, but now contextualizing it in the actuality of their experience.

Pastoral de conjunto is a rich and challenging term. Simple translation does not do it justice. Nevertheless, the need to convey its meaning, led to the formulation of a definition as used in the *National Pastoral Plan:*

> It is the harmonious coordination of all the elements of the pastoral ministry with the actions of the pastoral ministers and structures in view of a common goal: the Kingdom of God. It is not only a methodology, but the expression of the essence and mission of the church, which is to be and to make communion. (#6)

The literal translation which is sometimes offered in English is that of "organized pastoral effort." This definition seems to stress the practical dimension of the term. In order to understand the term in its fullness, it is important to reflect on the goal of *pastoral de conjunto.*

Goal of Pastoral de Conjunto

The primary concern of *pastoral de conjunto* in the task of evangelization is not pastoral efficiency. Its primary importance is that it is a methodology that places itself at the service of the

Kingdom of God and assists the faithful in its announcement and realization. It invites the people of God to commit themselves actively to continue the work of Jesus by entering into the cultural, religious, and social reality of the people, becoming incarnate in and with the people. The bringing about of the Kingdom that Jesus proclaimed is ultimately the goal of *pastoral de conjunto*. Everything that this pastoral concept and approach seeks to achieve has value insofar as it facilitates the carrying out of the mission of the church in making evermore present the Kingdom of God, a Kingdom furthered by the church's relentless preaching and testimony for the need of conversion, the affirmation of the dignity of the human person, and the seeking of ways to eradicate personal sin, oppressive structures, and forms of injustice (*National Pastoral Plan*, #6, 19-20).

In view of this common goal, pastoral ministers and structures are urged to place all of their efforts and existing resources in responding to this goal. However, this calls all pastoral ministers and structures to enter into communion among themselves; to move away from a posture of individualism and competition to one of harmonious coordination of all that they have at their disposal in order to further the goal—the Kingdom of God. Such action necessitates a conversion of persons and structures, a willingness to live the church as communion by entering into communion with each other. *Pastoral de conjunto is* then not only a methodology used to arrive at the goal, but a methodology to which one can be faithful only if it is grappled with in the context of daily living. To do otherwise is to suggest the erroneous belief that faith and daily life exist as two separate entities.

The Model of Church

As a result of living out the dynamism of *pastoral de conjunto,* the Hispanic people grows into an understanding of what model of church they desire. This model might be described as one in which everyone feels at home as in a family—where interpersonal relations and fraternal love are the norm and not the exception, a community wherein its members are supported in living their faith and in accepting the need for conversion. Communities of faith are nourished by prayer and made conscious of their responsibilities in society and to those in that society most in need. Such a church questions the injustice in society and accepts its responsibility to change it. The journey of a *Pueblo de Dios en Marcha* fleshes out for U.S. Hispanic Catholics a model of church which is communitarian, evangelizing, and missionary; incarnate in the reality of Hispanic people and open to the diversity of cultures; a promoter and example of justice; active in developing leadership through integral education; leaven for the Kingdom of God in society (*National Pastoral Plan,* #6, 19-20). This model of church can be promoted and lived by means of a *pastoral de conjunto.*

Contributions of U.S. Hispanic Catholics

The years following the convocation of the I Encuentro in 1972 provided Hispanics the time needed to deepen earlier insights that had resulted from their reflection on their social and pastoral reality. The result was the creation of pastoral concepts and terminology which gave expression to their experience as a people. The articulation of this experience of faith is a valuable contribution offered by Hispanics to the church and society. It is a contribution that integrates the best of Hispanic cultural values with those of the Gospel. This process of pastoral theologizing and implementation shows how cultural values can be placed at the service of the Gospel. It affirms the mystery of the Incarnation, and in doing so upholds the dignity of the human person and the uniqueness with which God blesses each culture. *Pastoral de conjunto* is a concept rooted in Gospel values and in the cultural values that a people espouse as ways of expressing what is most cherished in their relationship to others, to the world and ultimately to God.

The National Catholic Conference of Bishops issued a pastoral letter on December 12, 1983 entitled *The Hispanic Presence: Challenge and Commitment.* In it they indicated that Hispanics exemplify and cherish values central to the service of church and society. Among the values listed were those of profound respect for the dignity of each person, reflecting the example of Christ in the Gospels; deep and reverential love for family life, where the entire family discovers its roots, its dignity, and its strength; a marvelous sense of community; loving appreciation for God's gift of life (#3-4). These values have been nourished by God's Word and the life-giving images of Scripture. The flight into Egypt has special significance for those dispossessed. Jesus' concern for the blind, the lame, the imprisoned, the leper, the Samaritan woman are strong messages of the universality of the Kingdom of God and the respect owed to all. The constant invitation for unity expressed by God's Word—that all may be one—is lived out in the reality of the extended family. The extension of hospitality to the stranger and those in need is readily understood for a people who believe that the concept of family is all-inclusive. The existence of the family relies on its interdependence, and the gifts of each member are put to the service of the common good (1 Cor 12:12). The living out of these cultural values has enabled Hispanics to enflesh their model of church and to create the means to promote it—*pastoral de conjunto*.

Conclusion

In a society fragmented by individualism, competition, consumerism, violence, and blatant disregard for human dignity, the concept and methodology of *pastoral de conjunto* is a contribution that Hispanics make to the church and society. It calls for an interdependence of the faithful, based on genuine respect and regard for all. This requires an explicit affirmation of the concept of cultural pluralism in the church within a fundamental unity of doctrine (*Hispanic Presence, #2*). As a methodology, *pastoral de conjunto* moves the faithful toward communion and universality. It provides a pedagogy that requires continuous dialogue among the faithful as an essential dimension in pastoral planning. While it acknowledges the diversity of ministries within the church, it also underscores the mission of all the baptized to evangelize. The experience of living out *pastoral de conjunto* has shaped a model of church for Hispanics which integrates the best of their cultural values with that of Gospel values. Ultimately, *pastoral de conjunto* signals a model of church that implicitly recognizes both the sense of the faithful and hierarchical teaching as essential elements in the articulation of the faith (*Hispanic Presence, #13*). This in part marks the genius of U.S. Hispanic Catholicism.

TWENTY-ONE

Basic Christian Communities

Dolorita Martínez

Behind every pastoral attitude lies an image of church and a theological point of view. This determines, implicitly or explicitly, the spirituality and pastoral practice of the ecclesial community, orients its line of action and determines in final analysis its operative ecclesiology or model of church.

A church model is, therefore, the mode of being or the consequence of a way of being church at a specific moment in history; by the same token it determines a way to function as church. This double polarity of the image of church can also be explained as follows: the different steps it takes, the different positions or stances it assumes, the different statements it makes on behalf of or against an issue or problem, as well as the different attitudes it assumes at one time or another, result in creating a historical figure for itself.

The *National Pastoral Plan for Hispanic Ministry,* unanimously approved by the U.S. Bishops' Conference during their plenary assembly in Washington, D.C., in November, 1987, proposes a model of church in its General Objective:

TO LIVE AND PROMOTE. . .

by means of a *Pastoral de Conjunto*
a MODEL OF CHURCH that is:
communitarian, evangelizing and missionary
incarnate in the reality of the Hispanic people
and open to the diversity of cultures,
a promoter and an example of justice;

that develops leadership through integral education . . .
THAT IS LEAVEN FOR THE KINGDOM OF GOD
AND SOCIETY (#17)

In this pastoral objective is reflected an ecclesiology and a
pastoral approach that is unique and challenging. The pastoral
thrust that underpins this objective was actualized and encoded
within the *III Encuentro* Process wherein some 30,000 persons
throughout the country participated in small reflection groups.
Many of these small reflection groups were already permanent
Basic Christian Communities who were in fact living out this
model of church. Since the *III Encuentro* in 1985, many more
Basic Christian Communities have been born and continue to
incarnate the pastoral principles and ideals that this pastoral objective highlights.

The U.S. bishops, in affirming this pastoral objective and
the *National Pastoral Plan for Hispanic Ministry* as a whole,
are likewise affirming that the model of church which is being
enfleshed by the Basic Christian Communities (BCCs) or Small
Ecclesial Communities (SECs), cannot be considered simply another pastoral movement within the church; it is, in fact, the
church of Christ incarnating itself among the common people,
who through their faith response are establishing a dialectical
relationship with the world.

Terminology

It is difficult enough to arrive at a common name for Basic
Christian Communities, much less an agreed-upon definition.
The *National Pastoral Plan* uses the term "Small Ecclesial Communities"; however, at the level of pastoral practice one finds
different Hispanic communities using the names "Basic Christian
Communities" and "Basic Ecclesial Communities" as well. The
original name in Spanish, "comunidades de base," which comes
from the Latin American pastoral experience, is translated into
English as base communities or basic communities. Later the
word "eclesiales" ("ecclesial") was added to clarify that these basic communities were arising out of a common faith response

and were in fact the church incarnating itself among the common people.

One of the essential elements of Basic Christian Communities is that it is the church incarnating itself among the common people and arising out of a common faith response. Latin American theologians speak of this reality as "the church born of the people." This is not a denial of the fundamental truth that the church always arises out of an initiative "from above," from the Spirit who raises it up and from the Lord Jesus who convokes it. Nevertheless, at their more human dimension it can also be said that Basic Christian Communities constitute that most "fundamental portion" of the church which is truly present and operative at the most "basic" level of society.

It is this constitutive element of church that the *National Pastoral Plan for Hispanic Ministry* seeks to stress in choosing this more inclusive term: Small Ecclesial Communities. This model of church arises out of a common faith response in Christ and, through its dialectical relationship to the world, seeks to incarnate itself within the lived experience of the people. It may be said to have two basic ecclesial aspects or dimensions: one which will be referred to as "intra-ecclesial" the other as "extra-ecclesial." These Small Ecclesial Communities may be said to exist at once in the sphere of the church, as that "initial cell of the ecclesiastical structure and the focus of evangelization" and in a secular dimension at the basic level of society "as a point of departure for building a new society."

Varied Expressions

Basic Christian Communities are a growing phenomenon in all parts of Central and South America, the Philippines, southeast Asia, Africa, northern Europe, and the United States. The expression or pastoral practice embodied by Basic Christian Communities varies in many aspects precisely because the historical reality in which they are incarnating themselves is different, and also because of the emphasis that each chooses to place in the "intra-ecclesial" or the "extra-ecclesial" dimensions.

Basic Christian Communities began to take root within the Hispanic community in the United States as early as 1970. The

National Secretariat for Hispanic Affairs had coordinated two national symposiums or "encuentros" on "Comunidades Eclesiales de Base": the first one in 1978 and the second one in May, 1989. The developmental processes of Basic Ecclesial Communities have been analyzed at both of these *encuentros* and some general guidelines and ecclesiological principles articulated. The 1989 *Encuentro* also reaffirmed that the varied expressions of this model of church were all valid and valuable experiences.

The different expressions identified can be said to enter within a developmental continuum in which maturity and inculturation may be considered valid variables of comparison. At one end of the continuum, one finds Small Ecclesial Communities whose emphasis seems to be more on the "intra-ecclesial" dimension; generally these are well-organized communities whose focus is primarily around faith-sharing, Bible study and prayer. At the opposite end of the continuum one can find communities whose primary focus may be seen as "extra-ecclesial." These are generally communities who have been in existence for a few years; they generally have achieved a certain level of critical consciousness, are usually very active and often place great emphasis on social justice concerns. In between, one finds communities at different developmental stages. These stages are not necessarily or immediately related to the length of time a group has been together; more often the maturity depends on how and why the group came together in the first place.

The degree of inculturation that the group has achieved through critical reflection on their social reality promotes cohesiveness and gives the community a greater sense of purpose or identity. Through a process of reflection which one could describe as "confronting reality in the light of faith and Scripture," the group matures and becomes progressively more committed to liberative evangelization. All affirm the notion of community as flowing from the biblical people of God concept and evangelization as an ongoing process of conversion that calls them as individuals and as a Christian community to strive to effect a living synthesis of faith, justice and witness.

An Evangelizing Pedagogy

The Basic Ecclesial Community has been described by Brazilian José Marins as a new model of church, whose originality is primarily due to its methodology and priorities. The basic methodology that most of these communities follow is in fact an evangelizing pedagogy and can be outlined under four moments or developmental phases:

1. Confronting reality in the light of faith;
2. Creative response or commitment to action;
3. Broadening of the base;
4. Becoming church.

These four moments or phases do not necessarily happen independently of each other, but happen within a dynamic spiraling process. The level of consciousness and internal organization which directs this process varies according to the different communities. Also the actuality is far richer, more complex and fuller of irreducible detail than a schematically organized description can relate.

1. Confronting Reality in the Light of Faith

Small Ecclesial Communities are a way of becoming church. The focus of this first moment of this process is relational; it is also the level of faith development. The starting point is dialogue about what is important in life. It is the level at which the group decides to meet together regularly to develop a more personal and committed faith. Generally the group is formed by persons who have come to recognize the value of reflecting critically on their existential reality in the light of God's Word and who in turn invite others to join them in this process of reflection.

The basic thrust of this critical reflection is on two levels. First, there is the level of reflection on the concrete reality; that is, the reflection starts from questions or concerns that are raised by members of the community and that are touching their lives in some direct way. This is referred to as "reality analysis." Reality is complex and it encompasses everything: the cultural, social, historical, religious, economic and political. Within the process of reflection, reality is experienced as a series of concentric circles.

From an initial awareness of personal problems, members go on to discover those of the family, the neighborhood, the district, county and finally those of society in general. The issues and concerns that immediately motivate them are those affecting them directly, but as the reflection progresses they see the inter-relatedness of issues and problems.

At a second level or sub-moment of this reflection process, faith and the Christian perspective enters into play. Only after they have raised some concerns, aspirations, needs or problems, at a very real and human level, is the reflection directed toward the question of Christian response or commitment. God's Word in Scripture and a committed response is sought as a response to the lived reality. Sacred Scripture is thus historically situated, first by asking what the Apostolic community or Old Testament community understood the meaning of this text to be and what hope or teaching it may have had for them. On the basis of this textual analysis, a second set of questions is posed: How does this text—God's Word—become actualized for us today? How does this Word enlighten our reality? How does it challenge us? What vision and hope does it hold for us here and now? Reading Scripture from this perspective develops in the people a strong biblical faith and enables them to reinterpret their traditional faith critically in the light of their lived reality.

2. Creative Response and Commitment to Action

The second moment calls for a response. At this moment the community decides how it will concretize its response in faith with a specific action. The action is not chosen arbitrarily, but arises from communal reflection. This activity focuses the following criteria: Will it break down barriers of fear and feelings of helplessness? Will it build community? Will it develop new leaders? What will the community learn from this action? Will it give us a victory, however small, upon which to build later on? Is the action consistent with our values as followers of Christ?

3. Broadening the Base

This third phase or moment does not happen as an isolated moment but might be considered the maturing indicator that one sees as operative throughout the developmental process. As the participants' world vision is expanding and their faith commitment deepening, their base of operation is also widening. Since they are a faith community in dialectical dialogue with the world around them, they begin to take on greater challenges or actions that have a more global scope. An awareness of networking with other Small Christian Communities and with other organizations who also share some of their goals is also evident. This broadening of the base at the "grass-roots" level of society is also broadening the base of the "grass-roots" church.

4. Becoming Church

The awareness that their reflection group is "the church at the grass-roots' level" is something that happens in the process, not something that they define or set out intentionally to create. Small Ecclesial Communities do not come into being because people attend workshops on how to form community or on what it means to be "ecclesial." People form community when they share life experiences, seek to strengthen their faith and hope through Scripture reflections, celebrate their faith together, and concretely commit their faith to action. In the process of sharing their joys and sorrows, their struggles and simple faith, they become a believing people, the people of God. It is, likewise, in the process of evaluating where they are and where they have been that communities begin to articulate ecclesiological principles in their priorities and objectives.

Evangelizing Potential

The evangelizing potential of these Small Ecclesial Communities is clearly evident in the priorities and objectives that several fledgling communities articulated for themselves upon returning from the National Symposium on Small Ecclesial Communities, held in Washington, D.C., in May, 1989:

> We want and seek to be a part of the Church who is
> at the service of the Kingdom of God:

- prophetic, evangelizing and missionary communities that seek to become ferment in society; communities that are poor and of the poor, responsible and capable of speaking their own word at all levels of church and society;

- communities that are wholly ministerial, not clerical or authoritarian, but where ministry is exercised as service on behalf of the whole community;

- Christian communities committed to peace and justice, and the cause of liberation of all persons who are oppressed. . . .

We propose for ourselves the following objectives:

- to deepen our faith, reformulating it critically in the light of God's Word and our lived reality, recognizing and properly valuing the popular religion and traditions which are also part of our faith expressions;

- to strive to live the ideals of Christian love, which call us to communally share ourselves, seeking ever greater solidarity with our sisters and brothers who are poor and oppressed and who do not always feel welcome in our parishes;

- to strive for equality in every aspect of our communal prayer, study and sharing, and to commit ourselves to work for justice and equality both in the church and society;

- to celebrate our faith festively and communally, in relation to life's joys and hardships, seeking creative ways and symbols to help us articulate our faith and our struggles as a people: Pueblo de Dios en Marcha.

TWENTY-TWO

Reasons for Our Hope

Allan Figueroa Deck

ALMOST EVERY YEAR IN THE PAST DECADE AN ARTICLE OF MINE in America has described salient developments in Hispanic ministry—a record of crises and coming of age. In the recent past, I have been tempted to use the word "malaise," but even more recently, I have been, like C. S. Lewis, "surprised by joy."

The time has come, then, for an update on longstanding issues and trends in Hispanic ministry:

1) new insights into the success of evangelical and Pentecostal groups in attracting Hispanics;

2) the growing diversity among Hispanics in terms of national origin, social status, level of assimilation, and English or Spanish language acquisition;

3) a paradigm shift away from the "underclass" conception to a more balanced assessment of the Hispanic reality; and

4) new Hispanic leadership initiatives undertaken independently of the hierarchy.

Proselytism and Evangelization: An Exploratory Study, a project supported by the National Conference of Catholic Bishops and written by Sister Eleace King, I.H.M., of the Center for Applied Research in the Apostolate (CARA) at Georgetown University, details the extent of evangelical Protestantism's penetration of Hispanic and other immigrant groups. It also discusses the causes of, and possible responses to, this challenge. Sister Eleace's work is the best research yet attempted in the United States on this subject and provides one of the best bibliographies. Published in 1991, it has unfortunately been put on the shelf and is now collecting dust.

Are there now better understandings of the flight of Hispanics from their ancient Catholic faith than the ones suggested by the bishops' study? Perhaps one of the better insights, implicit in previous discussions (see, for example, "Proselytism and Hispanic Catholics: How Long Can We Cry Wolf?" *America*, 12/10/88) but now becoming explicit is this: the church is not *ministerially structured* to *attend* adequately to the huge numbers of baptized Hispanics.

The dominant Catholic concept of ministry places great emphasis on *priestly office* at the expense of a charismatic approach to ministry—one, that is, which stresses the baptismal call of the faithful and the corresponding need to identify and nurture gifts in the community. A new ministerial paradigm is required, one that empowers the faithful to assume real responsibility for a wide range of ministries. Vatican II encouraged a retrieval of this more balanced approach to ministry, but it has not occurred as widely or rapidly as needed to keep pace with the Hispanic demographic explosion.

Furthermore, a new reason for the movement of Hispanic Catholics to evangelicalism has recently been suggested by literature coming out of Latin America—namely, that deeper reflection prompted by the "crisis of utopia" in the wake of the Sandinistas' electoral defeat in Nicaragua and the fall of Communism worldwide. Surprisingly, this reflection has to do with the laudable but sometimes misguided efforts of Roman Catholic leaders to link faith with justice. According to these newer reflections, Hispanic Catholicism has always been a vehicle for the expression of popular aspirations within an oppressive social and ecclesial order. To serve this function, it developed indirect, symbolic ways to respond to, and sometimes even protest against, the harsh realities of life. The contemporary emphasis of progressive mainline Chris-

tians, Catholic and Protestant, on transformative action or "conscientization," has had the unexpected affect of "blowing the
cover" of Hispanics' historic way of dealing with oppression.

Researcher Jorge E. Maldonado, in "Building 'Fundamentalism' From the Family in Latin America" (Martin Marty and R.
Scott Appleby, eds., *Fundamentalism and Society,* University of
Chicago Press, 1993), suggests that the Latin American masses
find evangelical and Pentecostal Christianity more congenial than
the socially aware and analytically acute religion of pastoral
agents influenced by Leonardo Boff's latest writings. Evangelical
Christianity often (though not always) plays down the social implications of faith, remaining at the purely "spiritual" level.

For this reason, precisely, Maldonado believes that the
movement of Latin Americans to evangelical and pentecostal
Christianity is more significant than the movement of Catholics
and mainline Protestants to politically committed "base ecclesial
communities." According to him, liberation theology's influence
on the Latin American masses is less potent than that of evangelicalism and other new religious movements for the reason that
communities inspired by revolutionary praxis appear to be more
political than religious. This appearance discourages a struggling
people who instinctively and for seemingly good reasons (such as
preserving their lives) resist moving from *symbolic* to *overt* forms
of protest. If, as the Synod of Bishops proclaimed in 1971, "action on behalf of justice is a constitutive element of the preaching
of the Gospel," then appropriate, pastorally effective ways must
be found to establish that faith-justice connection—ways, however, that respect the people's sensibilities and experiences.

A second trend spotlights developments at home rather than in
Latin America: a more intense awareness nowadays of the rich
diversity of U.S. Hispanics. Concretely, there is a growing recognition of the need to diversify ministries. For instance, evangelization may be conducted in Spanish, in English or even in a bilin-
gual-bicultural fashion, depending on the particular group's level
of acculturation and language ability. Awareness of social class is
also necessary. An undifferentiated "option for the poor" on the
part of ministers can be interpreted as exclusivist, leading Hispan-

ics who happen to be upwardly mobile to regard themselves as outside the church's concerns.

Large migrations from the Dominican Republic to New York City and even to places as remote as Alaska have dramatized the changing character of the Hispanic presence, which is no longer merely a matter of Mexican Americans in the Southwest. Hispanics are now in virtually every section of the United States, and the Mexican presence, for example, is growing in Florida. Nicaraguans and Salvadorans have moved into Miami by the thousands, and Miami's "Little Havana" section is now called "Little Managua." While people of Mexican origin constitute the vast majority of Hispanics in the Los Angeles area, there are hundreds of thousands of Salvadorans, Guatemalans and Hondurans in that megalopolis. Hispanics are entering such northern climes as Minnesota and Wisconsin.

The decade of the 1980s witnessed the rise of this diverse Hispanic presence, and the word "Hispanic" or "Latino" was selected as an umbrella term. Outside the United States, there are really no Hispanics or Latinos. The very use of these terms refers to the emergence in the United States of a new consciousness, perhaps more fragile than some imagine, that seeks to assert an underlying unity based upon Latin American roots. Some call this the Hispanic Catholic ethos: the Spanish language, the syncretic mestizo or mulatto Catholic culture and, in many cases, the unfinished, common struggle for socioeconomic justice.

This newfound diversity of U.S. Hispanics, a diversity that includes social and economic mobility, raises yet another issue, the third trend worth noting. David Hayes-Bautista (*Burden of Support,* Stanford University Press, 1988; and *No Longer Minority,* U.C.L.A. Chicano Studies Research Center, 1992) reveals the inadequacy of the "urban underclass analogy" as applied to Hispanics, the tendency to conceive of Hispanics only in terms of deficits or dysfunctions: socioeconomic poverty, lack of schooling, social deviance and addiction. He points to a number of strengths discovered in the most recent research: strong family orientation, high labor participation, low welfare dependency, strong health indicators and strong educational improvement.

Hispanics have the highest rate of labor participation of any group in the country. They also live longer on the average than almost any other group. Hispanic children are among the most likely offspring of any U.S. group (including affluent Anglos) to live at home with mother *and* father. By the second generation, Hispanics advance educationally about as fast as mainline Anglos. In the prisons of California, moreover, Hispanics are represented proportionately to their percentage of the overall population. In light of these surprising findings, Hayes-Bautista pleads for a "paradigm shift" in how one conceives of Hispanics. His forthcoming book on the Latinization of California is part of an effort to turn people's thinking around on the Hispanic "problem."

How did society and the mass media get into this mental rut? For one thing, social science has tended to view Hispanics as it has viewed African Americans. In doing so, the academics compounded the error, for the multiracial character of Latino communities makes a racially-based focus inappropriate. Hispanics can be white, black, Native American or even Asian. Treating the Hispanics as a racial minority obscures the considerable mobility that Hispanics have in comparison with African Americans, who have continued to experience hypersegregation. While Hispanics often are segregated in urban barrios, they can and do move out. This has not been so noticeably the case for African Americans even more than 30 years after the civil rights legislation of the 1960s.

All of these factors point to the need to make distinctions and to acknowledge the diversity of persons of Latin American descent in the United States—insights that are forcing churches to do real *pastoral planning* and to move beyond simplistic understandings and old data. The successes of evangelical Christians can perhaps be credited to their insight into this diversity and their willingness to experiment in responding to that diverse presence creatively and energetically.

A fourth and particularly hopeful trend: Hispanic leaders are taking unprecedented initiatives in responding to the needs of their communities. There are many examples. In 1988 a group of

Hispanic theologians came together to form the Academy of Catholic Hispanic Theologians of the United States (ACHTUS). The academy has grown to almost 60 members from an original few. Its work was highlighted at the June 1993 annual meeting of the Catholic Theological Society of America in San Antonio, where the Rev. Virgilio Elizondo, a leading U.S. Hispanic theologian, gave a rousing keynote address. In November 1993, ACHTUS published the premier issue of the *Journal of Hispanic/Latino Theology*. Several members of ACHTUS have begun to publish, and in 1992 a kind of "boom" occurred: three anthologies of U.S. Hispanic theology. Notable in this "boom" are the contributions of Hispanic women such as Rosa María Icaza, María Pilar Aquino, Ada María Isasi-Díaz, Yolanda Tarango, Jeanette Rodríguez Holguín, Marina Herrera, Ana María Díaz Stevens, María de la Cruz Aymes and many others.

One secular Hispanic organization, the National Association for Chicano Studies, also offered several workshops on "Latino religion" at its 1993 annual convention.

In the past five years, major U.S. foundations such as the Lilly Endowment and the Pew Charitable Trust have provided seed monies for important new Hispanic projects. One of them is PARAL, Program for the Analysis of Religion Among Latinos, under the direction of Anthony M. Stevens-Arroyo of the City University of New York. In the fall of 1994 the University of Notre Dame Press published a three-volume historical study of Hispanics in the U.S. Catholic Church under the general editorship of Jay P. Dolan, who assembled a team of mainly Hispanic scholars to produce the most extensive history yet available on this topic. Scholars of Hispanic religion in the social sciences and theology are collaborating as never before.

In addition, thousands of Hispanic faithful are sharpening their pastoral skills. They have been exposed to Saul Alinsky-style community organizing based in parishes, an especially effective form of leadership development. One of the most prominent political leaders in the country, Gloria Molina, a Los Angeles County supervisor, began as a community organizer in her local parish. Hispanics like Gloria Molina are responding to the call to service in church and society as catechists, parish ministers and community and even political leaders. There are more than

1,200 Hispanic permanent deacons in the United States, and the number of Hispanic seminarians is steadily rising in several parts of the country, notably California and Texas. The number of Hispanic priests is slowly but perceptibly growing.

A new generation of Hispanics do not look first to the church or other institutions, but to themselves and to the family and local community. The idea that having Hispanic bishops in and of itself would provide a solution for Hispanic "problems" in the church is being left behind. While the need for more Hispanic bishops persists, many now look beyond that simple solution.

An interesting example at the grass roots is the National Catholic Council for Hispanic Ministry (NCCHM). Organizations like this one, independent of the hierarchy, were unthinkable in the Hispanic context of even a few years ago. Today NCCHM is regularly convoking a cross-section of Hispanic Catholic leadership, organizing a second national Hispanic Congress for 1996 similar to the 1992 "Roots and Wings" Congress, and spearheading a major national leadership development project. The bishops have cooperated in all of this, but have neither controlled nor funded it.

The Hispanic church of the future is arising. No longer will Hispanics be viewed as objects of concern, but rather as subjects and artisans of new developments in church and society. Trends point to an unprecedented movement of U.S. Hispanic Catholics out of the "sacristy" and onto the highways of American life. They bring to today's social and religious tasks a confidence and vision rooted in their centuries-old faith and culture.

APPENDIX ONE

Selected Pastoral Resources

Kenneth G. Davis

FOR READERS WHO WOULD LIKE MORE INFORMATION ABOUT A
particular topic related to U.S. Latino ministry, the following is a
list of pastoral aids grouped by theme. Each entry includes ex-
planatory but not evaluative remarks; while representative, the
list is not exhaustive. Some of the information may vary due to
personnel changes at various agencies and because some organizations are in rather precarious financial straits. However, the
National Catholic Council for Hispanic Ministry is an umbrella
association of some 50 national and regional organizations, including most of those listed below. For future information about
member groups or the congresses and studies NCCHM realizes,
contact them at 8601 Lincoln Blvd., Suite 320 A, Los Angeles,
CA, 90045. Phone and fax is (310) 649-4214. They publish a
newsletter called *Puentes.*

A source for national, regional, and diocesan ministry to
Hispanics is the Secretariat for Hispanic Affairs, 3211 4th Street
N.E., Washington, D.C. 20017-1194 or (202) 541-3150, FAX
541-3322. The Secretariat publishes a quarterly newsletter titled
En Marcha. Also the various regional and diocesan offices of
Hispanic ministry often privately publish valuable works and offer
workshops and seminars; they are a good source for information
pertinent to a particular locale.

Another resource which is not listed are diocesan newspa-
pers or newsletters. Among the largest are Washington, D.C.'s El
Pregonero, Miami's *Voz Católica,* Chicago's *Chicago Católico,*
and Los Angeles' *Vida Católica.* These and others can be found

in the handbook of the Catholic Press Association, 119 North Park Avenue, Rockville Centre, NY 11570, (516) 766-3400. The Catholic Publisher's Association offers *A Study of Religious Reading Needs Among U.S. Hispanic Catholics.* Their address is 333 Glenhead Road, Old Brookville, NY 11545.

Catechesis

Sister María de la Cruz Aymes, SH, internationally noted educator, and Francis J. Buckley, SJ published *Fe Y Cultura* through Paulist Press, 997 Macarthur Blvd., Mahway, NJ 07430 or (201) 825-7300.

The Hispanic Television Network produces a catalogue of over 50 Spanish language videos suitable for catechesis or group discussion for various age groups. Information from 130 Lewis Street, San Antonio, TX 78212 or 800-998-5955.

The National Catholic Education Association produced *Integral Education: A Response to the Hispanic Presence.* It is available from their offices at 1077 30th Street N.W., Suite 100, Washington, D.C. 20007-3852 or (202) 337-6232.

The National Organization of Catechists for Hispanics holds an annual meeting, publishes a newsletter, and is involved in various catechetical projects such as "Semillas del Reino." Their address is 531 Boden Way, Oakland, CA 94610.

Our Sunday Visitor publishes about three titles for children in Spanish. Some of their English-language material is supported by sample letters to parents in Spanish. Call or write 200 Noll Plaza, Huntington, IN 46750. 800-348-2440.

Sadlier has the most complete line of bilingual materials. Contact them at 9 Pine Street, New York, NY 10005 or 800-221-5175.

Sin Fronteras: Lineamientos para una Catequesis Evangelizadora was a joint effort by both Alta and Baja California to prepare an adequate catechesis, and catechists, especially for the border area. It will soon be available also in English. See St. Mary Press below.

Investigation

Apuntes is a bilingual quarterly containing rather brief articles and book reviews of import to the Hispanic Church. Send $10.00 for a subscription to the Mexican American Program, Perkins School of Theology, Southern Methodist University, Dallas, TX 75275.

Gale Research, Inc. of P.O. Box 33477, Detroit, MI 48232-5477 or 800-877-4253 carries a growing line of almanacs, directories, and other useful tools both in hard copy and CD-ROM. For information of almost any kind about U.S. Latinos, this is a good place to start.

The Parish Evaluation Project is a nine-page, bilingual questionnaire mailed to parishioners. The completed forms are then processed using the PEP software. This results in a report on the parish's demographics, attitudes, and participation. Write PEP at 2200 East Devon, Suite 283, Des Plaines, IL 60018.

Hispanic Link Weekly Report is a newsletter filled with breaking stories about Latinos. While expensive ($115.00 annually), its column "Collecting" often mentions free reports that can make up the cost. Write 1420 N. Street, N.W., Washington, D.C. 20005 or call (202) 234-0280, FAX 234-4090.

Since 1991 *Review for Religious* has published an annual article called, "U.S. Hispanic Catholics: Trends and Recent Works." Look for it in each March issue. Information from 3601 Lindell Blvd., St. Louis, MO 63108-3393 or (314) 535-3048, FAX 535-0601.

Also consult the "Guide to Organizations for Hispanic Affairs," found in *Strangers and Aliens No Longer,* available by calling 800-235-USCC. Ask for related titles.

The Spanish Speaking Bookstore has a knowledgeable staff and very complete catalogue. Contact them at 5127 North Clark Street, Chicago, IL 60640. Also (312) 878-2117 and FAX 878-0647.

The Theological Research Exchange Network is a user-friendly diskette and instruction booklet which allows one to access a large number of Doctor of Ministry projects from throughout the country. Several have been written about Hispanics and provide insight into some of the latest pastoral efforts in this area. Call 800-334-8736, FAX (503) 771-5108 or write P.O. Box 30183, Portland, OR 97230 for a free sample.

El Visitante Dominical is the only Catholic, Spanish, national newspaper. For $23.00 a year it is mailed weekly from P.O. Box 1130, San Antonio, TX 78294.

Liturgy

GIA Publications has several titles of interest, including music by Donna Peña and Cuco Chávez. Write 7404 South Mason Avenue, Chicago, IL 60638-6295 or 800-442-1358.

The *Instituto de Liturgia Hispana* is a national organization dedicated to the study and inculturation of the liturgy. Among its publication is the free newsletter *Amen.* Their conferences attract both prominent speakers and publishers. For information write P.O. Box 28229, San Antonio, TX 78228.

The Liturgical Press publishes a missalette, songbook, and over a dozen other titles for Latinos including the *Rito de la Iniciación Para Adultos,* as well as the scholarly *Journal of Hispanic/Latino Theology.* Call them at 800-858-5450 or FAX toll-free 445-5899. Their address is P.O. Box 7500, Collegeville, MN 56321-7500.

Liturgy Training Publications produces the lector formation series *Manual Para Proclamadores de la Palabra,* sacramental certificates, and various official liturgical documents in Spanish. It is all available from 800-933-1800 or 1800 North Hermitage Avenue, Chicago, IL 60622.

The Mexican American Cultural Center (MACC) publishes or distributes a number of titles, including some rituals unavailable elsewhere such as Angela Erevia, MCDP's *Quince Años,* and the bilingual *New Rite of Marriage.* Contact them at (210) 732-2156 or 3019 West French Place, San Antonio, TX 78228.

Oregon Catholic Press has a complete catalogue of Spanish language and bilingual books, recordings, and workshops. They also publish the quarterly magazine *Liturgia y Canción.* Call or write 800-548-8749; 5536 NE Hassalo, Portland, OR 97213.

J.S. Paluch re-enters the field by offering over 15 compositions of Mexican, Puerto Rican and Venezuelan style. One of their composers, Lorenzo Florián, also offers concerts and workshops. Ask about their liturgical calendar in Spanish, and bilingual bulletin service. For information, inquire at 3825 North Willow Road, Schiller Park, IL 60176 or 800-621-5197.

Migrants

The Catholic Migrant Farmworker Network can be contacted at P.O. Box 985, Toledo, OH 43696-0985 or (419) 243-6608. CMFN publishes a newsletter and conducts leadership training retreats and regional meetings.

People on the Move, and *En Marcha Hacía el Señor* are among the titles available through the office of the Pastoral Care of Migrants and Refugees, 3211 Fourth Street N.E., Washington, D.C. 20017-1194. Call (202) 541-3035 or FAX 541-3399.

Ministerial Formation

The Channing L. Bete Co., Inc. publishes a long list of colorful, illustrated booklets on many topics. They can be personalized and are available at volume discounts. Call 800-628-7733 or write 200 State Road, South Deerfield, MA 01373-0200. They will send free samples.

The Christophers' *News Notes* are free and available in Spanish. Contact them at 12 East 48th Street, New York, NY 10017 or (212) 759-4050.

Cuando el Tomar Ya No Es Gozar is a manual for training pastoral agents to recognize alcoholism and intervene in a culturally sensitive manner. It and many other Spanish language resources are available by calling the St. Anthony Messenger Press (which has merged with Franciscan Communications) at 800-488-0488 or writing 1615 Republic Street, Cincinnati, OH 45210.

Ethnic Communications Outlet offers some nine videos and the newsletter *Resonancia* for Hispanic ministry. Contact them at 4107 West 26th Street, Chicago, IL 60623 or (312) 522-5151.

Mensaje is a magazine about evangelization available from P.O. Box 1817, Kenner, LA 70063 or (504) 443-4612.

Senderos is the official bulletin of the Division of Hispanic Affairs of the California Episcopal Conference. It is available free from 1010 11th Street, Suite 200, Sacramento, CA 95814 and (916) 443-4851 or FAX 443-5629.

Servir Como Jesús by J. Juan Díaz Villar, SJ, and Segundo Galilea is available from the Centro Católico para Hispanos del Nordeste. Write to them about their other resources at 1101 First Avenue, Suite 1233, New York, NY 10022 or call (212) 751-7045, FAX 753-5321. MACC and the Southeast Pastoral Institute are, of course, other fine sources for ministerial workshops and retreats.

Orbis Books has published such readable works as Moises Sandoval's *On the Move: A History of the Hispanic Church,* and Virgilio Elizondo's *The Way of the Cross: The Passion of Christ in the Americas.* Call or write for a catalogue: Maryknoll, NY 10545. (914) 941-7636, FAX 945-0670.

The National Catholic Reporter is perhaps the best English-language weekly for reporting on Hispanics. See for instance their issue on "Fall Books" of 11 September 1992. The

NCR can be ordered by calling or writing: P.O. Box 419281, Kansas City, MO 64141, 1-800-333-7373.

Popular Religion

Arturo Pérez is a prolific author in this area. Among his books are *Popular Catholicism: A Hispanic Perspective,* distributed by The Liturgical Press.

Rezando el Rosario is a lavishly illustrated work by Alba House. Call or write for their entire line of titles: 2187 Victory Blvd., Staten Island, NY 10314.

Preaching

Editorial Caribe may be the best single source. They publish the multi-volume *Comentario Biblico Hispanoamericano* and also carry many titles such as Samuel Pagan's *Púlpito, Teología y Esperanza* and Orlando Costas' *Communicación por Medio de la Predicación.* Contact them at 800-322-7423 or 9200 South Dadeland Blvd, Suite 209, Miami, FL 33156.

La Palabra Entre Nosotros is published six times a year and includes meditations on the Scriptures for daily Mass, as well as articles which support the bimonthly theme. Subscriptions through 800-638-8539 or P.O. Box 826, Gaithersburg, MD, 20884-0826.

Para Meditar las Lecturas Dominicales is a monthly guide available in both Spanish and English appropriate for planning a homily within a small group experience. Contact Twenty-Third Publications, P.O. Box 180, Mystic, CT 06355 or 800-321-0411 for this and other titles.

"Reflexiones Sobre la Palabra" is part of the expanding bilingual newsletter *Nuestra Parroquia* published by Claretian Publications. They also publish *El Momento Católico,* a series on various pastoral themes. Call them at 800-328-6515 or write 205 West Monroe, Chicago, IL 60606.

Proselytism

Much of what has been written is by J. Juan Díaz Vilar, SJ, and available through the Centro Católico de Pastoral para Hispanos del Nordeste. These include his works, *Las Sectas*, and *The Success of the Sects Among Hispanics*.

See also *Respuestas Católicas a Preguntas Fundamentalistas* available through Liguori, One Liguori Drive, Liguori, MO 63057 or 800-325-9521, extension 635, FAX 800-325-9526. They publish many small, handy titles in Spanish, but also such items as the new catechism and a bilingual software package for creating bulletins which are more creative and didactic.

Hispanic is a good magazine to know about. Consult its November 1990 article by Vicki Larson, "The Flight of the Faithful," pages 18-23. For subscriptions call 800-251-2688 or write 985 San Jacinto Blvd., Suite 1150, Austin, TX 78701.

Vocation

Comunidades de Reflexión Eclesial Cubana en la Diáspora is an international movement of Cubans living outside of the Island. They conduct meetings to reflect on their reality, organize pilgrimages, and produce various publications. Contact them at P.O. Box 440022, Miami, FL 33144.

The Conference of Religious in Hispanic Ministry offers annual seminars and an occasional newsletter. Contact Clemente Barron, CP at 651 North Sierra Madre Blvd., Pasadena, CA 91107.

Las Hermanas is a national organization of Latinas. They publish a newsletter called *Informes,* hold conventions, and offer a support network. Write P.O. Box 15792, San Antonio, TX 78212-8992.

Serra International of 22 West Monroe Street, Chicago, IL 60603 published *God's Vineyard: Formation Program for*

Lay Vocation Ministers within the Hispanic Community in 1990.

See the magazine *Vocation and Prayer,* especially the July-September issue in both 1992 and 1993. 9815 Columbus Avenue, North Hills, CA 91343-9948 or (818) 893-4526, FAX 895-8934.

Youth

El Desafío de la Evangelización Juvenil Católica: Llamados a Ser Testigos y Narradores is a bilingual booklet from the National Federation for Catholic Youth Ministry and is available from Don Bosco Multimedia, 475 North Avenue, P.O. Box T., New Rochelle, New York 10802.

St. Mary's Press offers a new line of books for Latino youth. They can be contacted by writing 702 Terrace Heights, Winona, MN 55987-1320. Their free, quarterly, bilingual newsletter on youth ministry called *Construyendo Nuestra Esperanza* is available by writing 1737 West Benjamin Holt, Stockton, CA 95207. Ask about their new institute serving Latino youth.

The International Office of RENEW offers a series of five booklets for youth ministry in both English and Spanish. Other Spanish resources are also available. Ask for their publications list by calling 1-800-229-1232 or write 1232 George Street, Plainfield, NJ 07062-1717.

The Southeast Pastoral Institute (SEPI) has a retreat program and publications called *Pascua Juvenil.* That and other titles are available by contacting 7700 S.W. 56th Street, Miami, FL 33155 or (305) 279-2333, FAX 279-0925.

You Español! is a new magazine for Hispanic youth. Subscription information is available from (305) 569-0093 or 165 Madeira Avenue, Suite 6, Coral Gables, FL 33143.

About the Authors

Carmen María Cervantes was born in Mexico City and has lived for the last fifteen years in Stockton, California. Currently she is director of the Hispanic Youth Ministry Project for Saint Mary's Press and director of the *Instituto Fe y Vida,* a national institute of evangelization, formation, and leadership for Hispanic Catholics. She was one of the founders of the National Organization of Catechists with Hispanics and served two terms as its president. Carmen also has been closely involved with the National Catholic Council for Hispanic Ministry since its inception in 1990 and serves on its board of directors.

Kenneth G. Davis, OFM Conv., has worked in Hispanic ministry both in the United States and abroad for 15 years. Currently he is developing a Doctor of Ministry program focused on Latino pastoral care for the Oblate School of Theology in San Antonio, Texas.

Allan Figueroa Deck, SJ, teaches theology at Loyola Marymount University in Los Angeles and coordinates Hispanic pastoral programs in the Center for Pastoral Studies. He is also executive director of the National Catholic Council for Hispanic Ministry.

J. Juan Díaz Vilar, SJ, was born in Spain. He lives at St. Peter's College in New Jersey and is the founder of the evangelization program *El Dios de Nuestros Padres.* He works with evangelization leaders all over the United States.

Virgilio Elizondo is internationally known as a writer and speaker, particularly for his theological reflection on the Mexican-American religious experience. He is the founder of the Mexican American Cultural Center in San Antonio, Texas and was its first president from 1972-1987. For the past 12 years he has served as the rector of San Fernando Cathedral in San Antonio. Presently he is also the project director of the San Fernando Cathedral project, a study funded by the Lilly Endowment through MACC.

Angela Erevia, MCDP, is a ministry consultant and serves on the general council of the Missionary Catechists of Divine Providence. Her specialties include Hispanic faith expressions as they relate to evangelization, catechesis, and faith development.

Joseph P. Fitzpatrick, SJ, served for decades among the Puerto Rican community of New York and was a prolific writer on Puerto Rican Catholicism. At the time of his recent death, he was professor emeritus of sociology at Fordham University, Bronx, New York.

Alex García-Rivera was born in Cuba and raised in the United States. He teaches theology at the Jesuit School of Theology in Berkeley, California.

Ada María Isasi-Díaz is Associate Professor of Ethics and Theology at the School of Theology and Graduate School of Drew University in Madison, New Jersey. Born and raised in La Habana, Cuba, she does grass-roots research among Latinas across the United States in an ongoing effort to articulate a *mujerista* theology.

Alicia C. Marill was born in La Habana, Cuba and has worked with Hispanic youth in Miami for 22 years. Currently she is an adjunct professor of theology at Barry University and director of *Amor en Acción,* a lay missionary group of the Miami archdiocese. She also coordinates the pastoral outreach of *Amor en Acción* in the Dominican Republic.

Dolorita Martínez, OP, has twenty-five years' experience in Hispanic ministry at the diocesan, regional, and national levels and was one of the writers of the *National Pastoral Plan for Hispanic Ministry* (1987). Her vast experience in Hispanic ministry includes extensive work with *comunidades de base* in the United States and Latin America. Presently she is the general counselor for missions and ministry with the Dominican Sisters of Grand Rapids, Michigan.

Timothy M. Matovina recently completed work as associate project director of the San Fernando Cathedral project, a study funded by the Lilly Endowment through the Mexican American Cultural Center in San Antonio, Texas. Currently he teaches theological studies at Loyola Marymount University in Los Angeles.

Verónica Méndez, RCD, was born in Puerto Rico and raised in New York. She has served Hispanic communities from Florida to Chicago, including seven years as vocation director for Hispanics for the New York archdiocese. Presently she is the Director of Hispanic Ministry and Associate Dean of Formation at Mundelein Seminary in Mundelein, Illinois. She is also Mundelein's representative to the National Catholic Council for Hispanic Ministry and a member of the Executive Committee of the Conference of Religious for Hispanic Ministry.

Arturo Pérez Rodríguez has over 20 years of Hispanic pastoral experience in the Chicago archdiocese and is a past president of the *Instituto de Liturgia Hispana*. Currently he serves as an instructor at St. Joseph's Seminary and the Catholic Theological Union, both in Chicago, and is also a consultant for the Liturgical Studies Program at the Tepeyac Institute in El Paso, Texas.

Ana María Pineda, RSM, was born in El Salvador and raised in the San Francisco Bay area. She has extensive pastoral experience in Hispanic ministry at the parish, diocesan, regional, and national levels and is currently the Director of Hispanic Ministry at Catholic Theological Union in Chicago.

Yolanda Tarango, CCVI, serves in the leadership of the Sisters of Charity of the Incarnate Word and lives at Visitation House, a transitional residence for homeless women and children in San Antonio, Texas. She was national coordinator of *Las Hermanas* and part of the founding class of the National Hispana Leadership Institute.

Dominga Zapata, SH, is a native of Puerto Rico who has ministered from East Harlem to the Midwest. She is the Hispanic American Consultant in the Ethnic Ministries Office of the Chicago archdiocese and serves on the board of the National Catholic Council for Hispanic Ministry.

APPENDIX THREE

Sources

Cervantes, Carmen María. "Raices y alas de la evangelización de la juventud latina/Roots and Wings of the Evangelization of Latino Youth." *Construyendo Nuestra Esperanza* 5 (Summer 1992): 1-10.

Davis, Kenneth G. "Preaching in Spanish as a Second Language." *Homiletic* 17 (Summer 1992): 7-10.

Deck, Allan Figueroa. "The Crisis of Hispanic Ministry: Multiculturalism as an Ideology." *America* 163 (21 July 1990): 33- 36.

___. "Hispanic Ministry Comes of Age." *America* 154 (17 May 1986): 400-02.

___. "Hispanic Ministry: Reasons for Our Hope." *America* 170 (23 April 1994): 12-15.

Díaz Vilar, J. Juan. "Hispanics and the Sects in the United States." *Catholic World* 233 (November/December 1990): 263-65.

Elizondo, Virgilio. "Popular Religion as Support of Identity; A Pastoral-Psychological Case-Study Based on the Mexican American Experience in the USA." In *Popular Religion,* ed. Norbert Greinacher and Norbert Mette, 36-43. Edinburgh: T. & T. Clark, 1986.

Erevia, Angela. "Happy to Be Hispanic." *Religion Teacher's Journal* 25 (October 1991): 35-37.

Fitzpatrick, Joseph P. "The Hispanic Poor in a Middle-Class Church." *America* 159 (2 July 1988): 11-13.

___. "No Place to Grieve: A Honduran Tragedy." *America* 163 (21 July 1990): 37-38.

García-Rivera, Alex. "Let's Capture the Hispanic Imagination." *U.S. Catholic* 57 (July 1994): 34-35.

Isasi-Díaz, Ada María. "Hispanic in America: Starting Points." *Christianity and Crisis* 51 (13 May 1991): 150-52.

Marill, Alicia C. "Jovenes entre dos culturas/Youth Caught Between Cultures." *El Momento Católico* 29 (Chicago: Claretian Publications, 1992).

Martínez, Dolorita. "Basic Christian Communities: A New Model of Church Within the U.S. Hispanic Community." *New Theology Review* 3 (November 1990): 35-42.

Matovina, Timothy M. "Hispanic Catholics in the United States: No Melting Pot in Sight." *America* 164 (16 March 1991): 289-90.

___. "The Italian 'Problem' and the Hispanic Opportunity." *America* 165 (16 November 1991): 362-63.

___. "U.S. Hispanic Catholics and Liturgical Reform." *America* 169 (6 November 1993): 18-19.

Méndez, Verónica. "Vocation Ministry and Hispanics in the U.S.A." *Vocations and Prayer* 4 (July/September 1993): 5-11, 30-31.

Pérez Rodríguez, Arturo. "Hispanic Spirituality." In *The Modern Catholic Encyclopedia,* ed. Michael Glazier and Monika K. Hellwig, 828-30. Collegeville, Minnesota: Liturgical Press, 1994.

Pineda, Ana María. "Pastoral de Conjunto." *New Theology Review* 3 (November 1990): 28-34.

Tarango, Yolanda. "The Hispanic Woman and Her Role in the Church." *New Theology Review* 3 (November 1990): 56-61.

Zapata, Dominga. "The Caribbean Hispanic Contribution: A Puerto Rican Perspective." *Catholic World* 233 (November/December 1990): 257-62.